Todd English
and Sally Sampson

Photographs by Carl Tremblay

SIMON & SCHUSTER

THE OLIVES TABLE

OVER 160 RECIPES
FROM THE CRITICALLY
ACCLAIMED RESTAURANT
AND HOME KITCHEN
OF TODD ENGLISH

Simon & Schuster

Rockefeller Center

1230 Avenue of the Americas

New York, NY 10020

Text copyright © 1997 by Todd English and Sally Sampson

Photography copyright © 1997 by Carl Tremblay

SIMON & SCHUSTER and colophon are registered trademarks

of Simon & Schuster Inc.

Designed by Deborah Kerner

Illustration on page 208 by Carla Ventresca

Manufactured in the United States of America

10   9   8   7   6   5   4   3

Library of Congress Cataloging-in-Publication Data

English, Todd.

The Olives Table : over 160 recipes from the critically acclaimed

restaurant and home kitchen of Todd English / Todd English and

Sally Sampson.

p.   cm.

Includes index.

1. Cookery, Mediterranean.   2. Cookery, American.   3. Olives Table

(Restaurant).   I. Sampson, Sally, date.   II. Title.

TX725.M35E54   1997

641.59'1822—dc21   96-44532

CIP

ISBN 0-684-81572-9

To my wife, partner, and best friend, OLIVIA,
*and my three beautiful children—*OLIVER, ISABELLE, *and* SIMON—
and to my mother PATTY *for her encouragement to pursue this profession*

T.E.

To MARK, *without whom I would still be slaving over a hot stove
rather than a cold computer,
and to* LAUREN, *four, and* BENJAMIN, *two and a half, who can
identify and perfectly pronounce* tomatillo, focaccia, radicchio, arugula,
and cilantro *and can differentiate a Granny Smith apple from a Braeburn
apple and a clementine from a tangerine, based on taste alone*

S.S.

$\mathcal{A}$CKNOWLEDGMENTS

$\mathcal{W}$e gratefully thank:

Sydny Miner, our editor, who gave us an incredible opportunity. She has not only been an enormous support in writing this book but also its greatest fan.

Carl Tremblay, our photographer, whose patience, determination, and understanding allowed us to create such a beautiful book.

Carla Glasser, our wonderful and tireless agent, for listening to every idea and finding the perfect place to land.

T.E. and S.S.

A million thanks to:

Sally Sampson, my partner (or book wife, as I called her), for her always jovial spirit and perseverance in accomplishing the almost impossible task of writing this book with me. She is one of the most talented and accomplished writers I know.

My staff throughout the years:

Chefs Paul O'Connell, Marc Orfaly, Barbara Lynch, Paul Booras, Chris Moran, Joe Brenner, Ricky Gencarelli, Victor LaPlaca, Brad Stevens, Bob Sargent, Deb Merriam, Sara Jenkins, Christos Tsardounis, Bobby LaPorte, Liza S. Connolly, Dave Ogonowski, Judy Mattera, Paige Retus, and Dawn Rose.

Waitstaff and managers Jeff Nace, Danny Kogut, Lisa Kerr, Torri Crowell, Floyd Draeger, Albert Gaucher, Carla Gracey, Carla Ventresca, Bob Girardin, Rossana Cohen, Big Lou Zuluaga, Terry Ward, Dean Papandrea,

Larry Lester, Jody Duffin, Annie Copps, my faithful assistant Gina Gargano, and the late Patrick Alva and Kevin Hynes.

Bruce Cross (my Big Brother), who introduced me to Jean Jacques Rachou

Jean Jacques Rachou, for giving me my start. He was not only a mentor but a father figure as well

Michela Larson, for giving me my start in Boston and the opportunity to run her kitchen

Jasper White, for his encouragement to pursue my own thing and for his brotherly love.

T.E.

I'm forever indebted to Todd, who *really* taught me how to cook.

With love and thanks to my very own "diners' club" and Colleen Graham—without them a cookbook would be joyless and impossible.

S.S.

CONTENTS

TODD PUTS HIS WORDS ON A PLATE

SALLY: Where did you start in order to end up where you are today?

TODD: One night, when I was fourteen, I stopped by to see my friend Ivan. He was working at a little Mexican place in Branford, Connecticut, and he asked if I had plans for the evening—thinking he had something great in mind, I said that I had none. Instead, he said that his dishwasher was sick and asked if I could help out. There was no "dishwasher"; you washed pots and plates and silverware by hand. I just jumped right in and for some strange reason, I really loved it. I don't know why—well, okay, you got as much free beer as you wanted.

SALLY: Seriously. . . .

TODD: There was a family feeling that I liked. There was energy and camaraderie and at the end of the night, a great sense of accomplishment. I liked it so much that when Ivan offered me the job, I took it and washed dishes for three to four months. When I turned fifteen, I got promoted to prep cook and made chips and meat sauce and chopped whatever was needed for the next day. I continued working all through high school.

SALLY: Is cooking in your blood?

TODD: Definitely. Well, I haven't always had the confidence to believe that it was there because I'm the kind of person who watches and observes and learns but in the end, I have to do it my own way. That's scary, because I'm always throwing myself out there rather than relying on the tried and true.

When I was a child we used to visit my great-grandmother, Bettina, and my great-grandfather, Rosario, in their home in Kent [Connecticut]. I remember going in their small, dark bedroom and seeing pasta drying on her bed. She rolled pasta dough around a knitting needle to make tubular pasta. She also made little ravioli and gnocchi. She let me stand on a stool next to her and show me what she was doing. Bettina was from Calabria and there were always lots of tomato-based meat braises and roasts. We ate antipasto first, then a pasta dish, and then a roast or a meat. Quintessential Italian cooking. She used to let me sip off the wooden spoon—I can still taste those sauces in my mind.

I took home economics in high school, but I only went to two classes. We made cakes from boxes, and I went straight to the counselor and said, "This class is not for me, I don't make cakes from boxes." I knew in my heart that it wasn't right.

SALLY: Why did you go to cooking school?

TODD: I took cooking very seriously. It made sense to formalize what I had learned, but I didn't really know what I was getting into. I learned early on that you get out what you put in and I happened to be ready to go in 100 percent. Actually, I realized how little I really knew.

I went to the CIA [Culinary Institute of America] because it had the best reputation. What you can gain in ten years of experience, you can get in two years of schooling. But it's not practical experience. They have state-of-the-art equipment, especially at Greystone [the new facility in Napa Valley] but, let's face it, it's not reality. Chances are that you graduate and get a job in a really nice restaurant and work on a range that you have to light with a piece of paper or the burners get clogged or your mise en place is floating in a pool of melted ice. The reality is that you're not working in perfect conditions but you have to perform as if you were.

SALLY: When you hire a cook, do you care whether they've gone to cooking school?

TODD: It helps, but it's not absolutely essential. It shows a commitment to cooking as a profession, but I don't think that the only good cooks come out of cooking school. The more perspective you have, the better. Cooking is an interpretation of one's experiences and one's knowledge.

Without schooling, what I'm interested in is that they've had some experience and are willing to learn. I also want people who have an athletic background, because it enables them to have an understanding of teamwork. It also means they have stamina, good hand-eye coordination, agility, and the drive to be in shape, all qualities that help in a kitchen. At least in mine.

SALLY: What's the difference between an okay cook and a great one?

TODD: You've got to love being a cook. You either dive into it and you live it and breathe it and dream about it or you don't. You have to have the drive and you have to have something to prove. Part of being a great cook or chef is knowing who you are and what you're about.

SALLY: There was a time when being a chef was not as appealing as it is now. Now, being a chef is not only well respected but glamorous, even sexy.

TODD: There's a certain energy you get while cooking. It probably makes you exude endorphins. It's a high that's kind of sexy when things are really pumping and you're feeling creative. Other than great sex, there's nothing like it. It's a kind of excitement that's addictive. I've talked to a lot of chefs about this— we're all junkies on this high, which is probably why we do what we do and work the kind of hours we work.

SALLY: Are you talking about the thrill that comes from being in the limelight?

TODD: No. I hope that glamour isn't what attracts people to becoming chefs. If you're in it for the glamour, that's the wrong reason. You're not going to last; you've got to love it.

SALLY: What was it like working at La Côte Basque [in Manhattan] in its heyday?

TODD: I have never been so nervous in my life. I used to wake up sick to my stomach. I was terrified that I couldn't perform. I had never stepped foot in a kitchen quite like it. Either you ran and jumped on the fast train or you got off. So I ran and ran.

La Côte Basque had just reopened with Jean-Jacques Rachou as the chef and he was doing a combination of nouvelle and classical cuisine. At that time, nouvelle was Rolled and Poached Sole with Kiwi Slices and lots of raspberry sauces. Salmon with Mango Beurre Blanc. I liked his rustic dishes best.

Like cassoulet, osso buco, and simple roasted chicken. I loved his sense of aesthetics. I got a lot of practical training, not only in the classical sense but also in production, because we really had to crank it out.

SALLY: Were you married then?

TODD: No, Olivia and I got married in 1986. We met in 1982, when we were both students at the CIA. I took her picture for her school ID. You know, love at first snap. She cooked for a while but I don't think she ever really loved it. We moved to Boston in 1984 to work with Michela [Larson, owner of the former Michela's in Cambridge, Massachusetts] and when the opportunity came for her to run the front, she grabbed it. Olivia knew that it was the better fit for her and with our personalities, it was better for us not to compete. I got the job as the sous chef and went off to Italy for a while to study Italian cooking.

SALLY: Cooking in restaurants in Italy must have been an incredible experience in every way.

TODD: When I came back from Italy, I knew that even though I wanted to be authentic, it wasn't going to work for the American palate. I used northern regional cooking as a base and went on to discover my own interpretation of what I had seen and tasted. For example, we would take a simple roast loin of rabbit with a balsamic vinegar glaze, then serve it over polenta and with roasted radicchio and some sort of green. In Italy you would be served these dishes on three separate plates, but we served them all on one, layering the flavors.

SALLY: So when people see your food, they think it's very wacky when in fact . . .

TODD: . . . it's traditional. When I cook, I believe in evoking some sort of memories. Some people are more adventurous and some are more staid. Some people live to eat and some eat to live, but when it comes down to it, everyone is looking for a certain sensation: food is to satisfy your soul. But it has to have a combination of comfort, refinement, and newness.

SALLY: And yet today you made a great simple grilled scallop dish and you had to add another level to it, a walnut paste, and then put that on top of something else. Each element may be simple, but what you do is not exactly simple when it's all said and done.

TODD: Olives is about the foods that you don't eat on a normal basis. Recognizable and yet foreign. The scallop dish: chances are, if I'm eating the scallops at home I'm going to eat them alone, but in the context of Olives and this cookbook, it's making things that are a little more special.

SALLY: You don't want people to eat at Olives and walk away and say, "I could do that," and yet aren't you instructing them to with this cookbook?

TODD: Well, there's still nothing like eating out. But more seriously, the more knowledge we have of food (or anything), the more sophisticated we become and the better things will be. I want this book to enable people to take simple ingredients and make them more interesting, more elaborate, more fun.

SALLY: How did Olives evolve?

TODD: It was time to leave Michela's. It had been three years and I knew I wanted to do my own thing. I left in October and we had a thousand dollars in the bank; we had one month to figure out what we were going to do. We started catering, and by December we had made enough money to go to Europe for two weeks. We gathered ideas and things for the restaurant, including three thousand dollars' worth of copper pots, although we still didn't have money or a location. By February we found a location and we got a bank loan, and on April twenty-seventh we opened up.

SALLY: Why the name Olives?

TODD: I had just seen my uncle and he talked about the olive farms in Italy that my great-great-grandparents had owned. At first we thought we might call it Oliva ("olives" in Italian) or Olivia (after Olivia), but we decided on Olives and to keep the name American because we were in America. The whole concept of Olives was of cooking food from where olives grow. The whole Mediterranean belt.

This idea had been brewing inside me for a long time. I had dreamed about it. I wanted to do a wood-burning stove and a rotisserie. We wanted to model it after the neighborhood bistros in France and the family trattorias in Italy. The places I remember the most are not the three-star restaurants, but the ones off the beaten path—the secret, undiscovered places with quality food and excitement.

SALLY: You may have modeled yourself after that but that's not really Olives, is it?

TODD: We were for a while, and in a way, we still are. I think of myself that way. What makes these restaurants great is that they have a clear definition of what they are, and I believe that it gives them longevity. And that is what Olives is.

When we opened we were like a ma-and-pa restaurant: open kitchen, fifty seats, me cooking. Olivia in front, one other cook, and two waiters. We started out with very rustic, undertoned country cooking. As our clientele base grew, they demanded more and more refinement and it made me discover just how far I could go with the food.

SALLY: What was on the first menu and how did you decide upon it?

TODD: There were a few classic things that I just wanted to have—like spit-roasted chicken—and it just grew from there: tortelli with butternut squash and the Olives tart. Pizza. Roasts and whole fish. I had never worked with a brick oven before and I was really excited about it and I just cooked and cooked and cooked.

SALLY: What happened the first day that you opened?

TODD: The first day, we invited neighborhood people and friends in as our guests. I think it was a Saturday and we closed Sunday and Monday and finished painting the walls. We opened on Tuesday to about a hundred people and it just never stopped. It was wild.

I'll never forget our first really big night. Just Paul [O'Connell, now the chef/owner of Providence, in Brookline, and Chez Henri, in Cambridge] and I were cooking. We cooked for about a hundred and forty people. Michela and Jasper [White, chef and owner of the former Jasper's, in Boston] and Jimmy [Burke, chef and owner of the Tuscan Grill, in Waltham] all came in. It seemed like the whole restaurant community was there.

SALLY: You weren't prepared for that?

TODD: No. In fact, I designed the kitchen so that I could do it myself. If no one came, it wasn't going to be a big problem. I could reach everything standing anywhere. I could reach the grill, the stove, the oven.

SALLY: Who do you respect in the food industry?

TODD: Fredy Girardet [a famous three-star chef in Switzerland], because he has a reputation for being the best at what he does. The Troisgros brothers. Some of the older chefs who have practiced their craft for so many years. People who are always changing and evolving.

SALLY: What do you like to eat?

TODD: Fresh-squeezed orange juice. Dark-roasted coffee. Sandwiches—there's something cool about eating foods with your hands. Smoked salmon and poached eggs on Sunday morning, although not necessarily together. I'm intrigued with mustards. I always try to keep pasta and good canned beans around. Grilling fish in the summer. I love peanut butter and jelly.

SALLY: Welch's grape?

TODD: High-quality cherry preserves. Blueberry preserves.

SALLY: What's dinner like in your house?

TODD: Chaotic. The truth is, I'm never there. I don't know. I mean I hear it's chaotic.

SALLY: What's your favorite thing to cook?

TODD: Rabbit. It is the most elegant meat there is.

SALLY: Your favorite thing to eat in a restaurant?

TODD: Sushi. Number one, because it's so different from what I do. I've always had a fantasy of opening up a sushi restaurant. And number two, it's pure, clean, and simple, in a certain way.

SALLY: What influences you the most?

TODD: I don't know. I get a lot of ideas from traveling. I recently went to Israel and when I came back, I started cooking a lot of different hummus dishes. I reinterpreted a lot of what I saw or infused it with my own style.

I love reading old cookbooks. And the cookbooks of my peers, but I try to envision my own thing.

SALLY: Which is? Can you describe it?

TODD: How do you answer that question? It's Mediterranean-inspired. It's layered, complex. It's refined rustic.

SALLY: A contradiction in terms.

TODD: I like to reinterpret, but I think that what is most important in cooking is the personal side. That's the beauty and the art of it. You can't be afraid of it—I'm more able to express myself that way and take more chances. The thing about cooking is that you really put your heart and soul on the plate.

It's interpretive Mediterranean cooking. The ingredients are from here, but I rework them with a Mediterranean sensibility: taking what you have from down the road and cooking it.

SALLY: Can you cook Mediterranean food without Mediterranean ingredients?

TODD: Absolutely, although I don't think you can cook it without olive oil.

SALLY: How do you feel about people who say that something you make isn't authentic and traditional?

TODD: Tradition provides guidelines. It's a good start and there are reasons things were done a certain way. But . . . I can make something authentic and it may not taste good. If it's authentic and it's good, then I will make it authentic, but if it's authentic and I think I can make it better, then I will.

SALLY: So, what's the bottom line?

TODD: I've been studying for fifteen years, I've traveled to many places and sampled lots of cultures and cuisines. The true heart and soul of food should not be overintellectualized to the point where food becomes cerebral. The most important thing is that food should taste good, and that's something you just feel. Once you begin to feel it, you won't ever have to think about it again and it just becomes natural. After all, it's only food.

THE OLIVES PANTRY

*T*he basis of the cooking at Olives is taking common ingredients and re-arranging them in a way that makes them uncommon and interesting. In addition, it is providing an atmosphere around the food that creates excitement and entertainment. Having a fully stocked pantry will enable you to duplicate my recipes, but the atmosphere is up to you.

DRY GOODS

ANCHOVY FILLETS, CANNED BOTH IN OIL AND IN SALT

ARTICHOKE HEARTS AND BOTTOMS, CANNED

BAKING CHOCOLATE *(I use Callebaut or El Rey)*

BAKING POWDER

BAKING SODA

BALSAMIC VINEGAR

BROWN SUGAR, DARK AND LIGHT

CANNELLINI BEANS, DRIED OR CANNED

CHICK PEAS, CANNED

COCOA POWDER *(I use Droste or Callebaut)*

FLOUR, ALL-PURPOSE

HONEY

LENTILS, DRIED, BROWN

MUSTARD, GRAINY AND SMOOTH DIJON

OATS, ROLLED
OLIVE OIL, VIRGIN AND EXTRA-VIRGIN
PASTA, ASSORTED SHAPES
RICE, BASMATI AND SUPERFINO ARBORIO
SALT, KOSHER
SEMOLINA
SESAME TAHINI, CANNED
TOASTED SESAME OIL
TOMATOES, CANNED WHOLE AND CRUSHED
TOMATO PASTE
VIETNAMESE CHILI PASTE
WHITE SUGAR
WINE, RED AND WHITE

DRIED SPICES

Spices are best purchased in their whole, natural state rather than preground. At Olives, whenever possible, we grind our own spices in a coffee grinder, which results in a spice with more perfume. If you cook a lot, you'll find that it's worth having one grinder designated specifically for this use.

BAY LEAVES
CARDAMOM PODS
CAYENNE
CINNAMON, GROUND AND STICKS
CUMIN SEEDS, WHOLE OR GROUND
CURRY POWDER
FENNEL SEEDS, WHOLE
GINGER, GROUND
NUTMEG, WHOLE OR GROUND
PAPRIKA, HUNGARIAN
PEPPERCORNS, BLACK
RED PEPPER FLAKES, CRUSHED

SAFFRON THREADS
TURMERIC
VANILLA BEANS, TAHITIAN
VANILLA EXTRACT

FRUITS AND VEGETABLES

CARROTS
CELERY
GARLIC
GINGER
LEMONS
LIMES
ONIONS, SPANISH AND RED
POTATOES, IDAHO AND NEW
TOMATOES, BEEFSTEAK AND PLUM
SHALLOTS
SWEET POTATOES

REFRIGERATOR

BUTTER, UNSALTED
CORNMEAL, STONE-GROUND YELLOW
OLIVES, ASSORTED
PARMESAN CHEESE *(in a chunk)*
ROMANO CHEESE *(in a chunk)*

FREEZER

BUTTER, UNSALTED
BACON, SLAB
PEAS

THE OLIVES KITCHEN

*H*aving good equipment won't make you a good cook, but it will make your life easier. Here's a list of what I don't like to do without.

BLENDER

CHARCOAL, HARDWOOD

CHEESE GRATER

METAL FLUE *(chimney)—a cylinder made of sheet metal that you fill partway with newspaper and then top with charcoal; it ignites the charcoal faster than if you place it directly in the pit.*

COFFEE GRINDER

COLANDER

CUTTING BOARD *(a big heavy wooden one that won't move around)*

FOOD PROCESSOR

GRILL, CHARCOAL OR WOOD-BURNING *(not gas)*

JAPANESE MANDOLINE—*a mandoline is a cutting and slicing device, somewhat like a grater, with adjustable blades for slicing and cutting into julienne or thicker matchsticks. It makes it easy to achieve a consistent, uniform shape. There are French, German, and Swiss mandolines on the market but we like the Japanese because it does a great job, is inexpensive, and is readily available in Asian markets.*

LADLES
MEASURING CUPS
MEASURING SPOONS
MIXING BOWLS, STAINLESS STEEL
MORTAR AND PESTLE
POTATO MASHER
ROTISSERIE *(optional)*
SIEVE
SLOTTED SPOONS
SPATULAS
TONGS
VEGETABLE PEELER
WHISKS
WOODEN SPOONS

POTS AND PANS

8-QUART STOCKPOT
8-INCH HEAVY CAST-IRON SKILLET
10-INCH HEAVY SKILLET
14-INCH HEAVY SKILLET
SAUTÉ PANS, 7-INCH AND 10-INCH

KNIVES

8-INCH CHEF'S
9- OR 10-INCH SLICING
BONING
PARING
SERRATED BREAD

$\mathcal{B}$ ASICS ·

■ *The following recipes are not basic to everything I cook, but they are called for in a lot of my recipes. When I was in cooking school, we were taught basic "mother sauces," most of which no longer apply to contemporary cooking. Included in this chapter are the few that I still use.*

ROASTED GARLIC

If you've ever eaten at Olives, you know that garlic is the foundation for all I cook. In fact, if I were ever to change the name of the restaurant, it would be to Garlicks. It is the one and only ingredient that I could not do without. My love affair with garlic has existed as long as I can remember. I can still feel and smell my great-grandmother grabbing me lovingly by the chin—and then nearly fainting from the pungency of the garlic oil on her hands. Later, I can remember the smells and sounds of the garlic crackling as it hit the hot olive oil in her large blackened sauce pot. Whether by nature or nurture, I always have the rich smell of garlic emanating from my fingers. (Sorry, kids!)

Roasted garlic makes a great spread for toasted bread, but my favorite way to use it is to add it to stocks and sauces, such as a reduced chicken stock, in order to thicken them. Thickened this way, the stock intensifies the flavor of dishes such as Garlic-Lobster Risotto Calabrese (page 198). It also makes a great broth for steaming mussels and littleneck clams. Add roasted garlic cloves to mashed or baked potatoes or smash them into the skin of a roasted chicken or a grilled steak.

■ *Always buy the freshest garlic you can find: the fresher it is, the sweeter it will be. The best garlic has firm, tissue-like skin and should not be bruised, sprouted, soft, or shriveled. If you find cloves that have tiny green shoots, be sure to discard the shoots: they will only add bitterness.*

MAKES 2 GARLIC BULBS

2 garlic bulbs, unpeeled, tops sliced off
2 tablespoons olive oil
½ teaspoon kosher salt
¼ teaspoon black pepper

Preheat the oven to 400 degrees.

Place the garlic bulbs in a small baking dish and sprinkle with the oil, salt, and pepper.

Bake, uncovered, until the garlic is lightly browned and soft, about 25 minutes. When following this recipe to make roasted shallots, bake for 50 minutes. Use immediately, or store in the refrigerator for no more than 1 week.

■ *SALT TALK*

I hate iodized salt, which is way too salty. I know that sounds strange but it is and I recommend, instead, kosher salt. The sole purpose of salt is to enhance the flavor of food (by bringing out its sweetness or giving food a nice crust) rather than to make it salty. How do you tread this fine line? Follow our recommendations for salt. We tested every single recipe.

ROASTED VIDALIA ONIONS

I love onions. Probably the most democratic vegetable on earth, they cross every border and culture. I can think of no cuisine that does without them—and I certainly wouldn't want to.

Roasting is a wonderful alternative to sautéing onions. It adds another dimension to the flavor, making the onions both sweeter and richer. These onions can be sliced and substituted for sautéed onions in any dish or used for Pan-Roasted Rib Eye with Gorgonzola Vidalia Onions (page 258) or in Roasted Onion Soup (page 102). Or simply serve them as a side dish drizzled with Walnut Romesco (page 47). If using for the soup, add to the sautéed leeks and proceed.

MAKES 4 ONIONS

4 Vidalia, Bermuda, Walla Walla, or Texas Sweet onions,
*   unpeeled*
1 tablespoon olive oil
2 tablespoons chopped fresh rosemary leaves or 2 teaspoons
*   dried rosemary*
1 teaspoon kosher salt
½ teaspoon black pepper

Preheat the oven to 450 degrees.

Sprinkle the onions with the oil, rosemary, salt, and pepper. Place in a roasting pan or heavy skillet in the oven and roast for 20 minutes. Reduce the heat to 250 degrees and roast for an additional 45 minutes.

When the onions are cool enough to handle, peel them. They can be used immediately or refrigerated for up to 1 week.

ROASTED TOMATOES

*T*his is a great way to concentrate the flavors of the tomato, and if you want to blister the skin, broil for 3 minutes at the end.

MAKES 12 TOMATOES

12 plum tomatoes
1 tablespoon olive oil
1 teaspoon kosher salt
½ teaspoon black pepper

Preheat the oven to 250 degrees.

Place the tomatoes on a baking sheet and rub with the oil. Sprinkle with the salt and pepper.

Bake until the tomatoes are shriveled and slightly darkened, about 3 hours.

CROUTONS

*M*y cooks accuse me of having a "problem" with croutons. I often find myself munching on one without even knowing it. Crunchy and browned on the outside and a little chewy on the inside, they're irresistible.

6 to 8 cups ½-inch bread cubes
2 tablespoons olive oil
1 to 2 garlic cloves, minced
½ teaspoon kosher salt
¼ teaspoon black pepper
2 tablespoons finely grated Parmesan cheese

Preheat the oven to 350 degrees.

Place the bread cubes on a baking sheet and sprinkle with the oil, garlic, salt, pepper, and cheese. Bake until they are golden, about 15 to 20 minutes.

SHALLOT VINAIGRETTE

A vinaigrette should enhance, not mask, whatever it is paired with. This version is our basic vinaigrette. Serve it on a chopped red onion and fresh tomato salad, cold leftover steak, or a salad of carrots, celery root, and asparagus.

MAKES ABOUT 1½ CUPS

1 shallot (raw or roasted according to the instructions for Roasted Garlic,
*   page 28, doubling the roasting time to 50 minutes)*
1 tablespoon Dijon mustard
½ cup balsamic vinegar
½ teaspoon kosher salt
½ teaspoon black pepper
1 cup extra-virgin olive oil

Place the shallot in a food processor fitted with a steel blade and pulse until minced. Add the mustard, balsamic vinegar, salt, and pepper and pulse until combined. While the machine is running, gradually add the olive oil in a thin, steady stream, and process until smooth.

The vinaigrette keeps for 2 to 3 days.

GARLICKY SALAD DRESSING

This is another all-around salad dressing, great on mesclun greens or a salad of romaine and Parmesan cheese. Use it for marinating vegetables and for drizzling on grilled fish or chicken.

- *One half-teaspoon anchovy paste is equal to 1 anchovy fillet, chopped.*

MAKES ABOUT 1½ CUPS

2 garlic cloves, finely chopped
½ cup fresh lemon juice (about 2 lemons)
1 cup extra-virgin olive oil
½ teaspoon anchovy paste
½ teaspoon kosher salt
¼ teaspoon black pepper

Place the garlic, lemon juice, olive oil, anchovy paste, salt, and pepper in a blender and process until smooth.

The salad dressing keeps for 2 to 3 days.

Spicy Aïoli

There is a common theme of these sorts of "mayonnaise-y" sauces throughout the Mediterranean: the Greeks have Skordalia, the Spanish have Romesco, and the French have Aïoli. Although Aïoli is traditionally made with tons of garlic, in this version the strongest flavor is an ingredient other than garlic: chile pepper. This is not something you'll want to eat in large quantities, but it's a great way to spice up a dish.

Spicy Aïoli is great on everything from French fries to baked potatoes to grilled fish to soft-shell crabs. This recipe can be easily halved.

MAKES ABOUT 2 CUPS

3 garlic cloves
¼ cup fresh lemon juice (about 1 lemon)
½ cup fresh bread crumbs
2 large egg yolks
1 teaspoon chopped jalapeño or Scotch bonnet pepper
1 teaspoon ground cumin
1 teaspoon minced peeled fresh ginger
½ teaspoon Hungarian paprika
1 teaspoon kosher salt
½ teaspoon black pepper
½ cup water
1½ cups olive oil

Place the garlic, lemon juice, bread crumbs, egg yolks, jalapeño pepper, cumin, ginger, paprika, salt, and pepper in a blender and process for 1 minute, or until everything comes together in a chunky paste. Add the water and process to mix.

While the machine is running, add the oil in a thin, steady stream and process until smooth.

CITRUS AÏOLI

Citrus Aïoli is good on grilled fish, chicken, oysters, or shrimp. I like it in tuna salad instead of regular mayonnaise.

MAKES ABOUT 1½ TO 2 CUPS

2 garlic cloves
Grated zest and juice of ½ lime
Grated zest and juice of ½ orange
Grated zest and juice of ½ lemon
½ cup fresh bread crumbs
2 large egg yolks
½ teaspoon Hungarian paprika
½ teaspoon kosher salt
½ teaspoon black pepper
1 tablespoon water
1¼ cups olive oil
¼ cup finely chopped fresh cilantro leaves
¼ cup finely chopped scallions

Place the garlic, citrus zest and juices, bread crumbs, egg yolks, paprika, salt, and pepper in a blender and process for 1 minute. Add the water and process to blend. While the machine is running, gradually add the oil in a thin, steady stream and process until smooth. Stir in the cilantro and scallions.

Saffron Aïoli

When I was in Spain, I was invited to pick saffron, but I decided simply to watch. I couldn't believe what a pain in the butt it was. Since then, I've stopped complaining about the prices I once thought to be exorbitant.

Saffron has a heady, rich, spicy, floral, citrusy, and aromatic lusciousness to it that is the greatest complement to any kind of fish stew or other fish dish.

ABOUT 2 CUPS

1 generous teaspoon saffron threads
1 cup water
3 garlic cloves
1 teaspoon kosher salt
½ teaspoon black pepper
¼ teaspoon cayenne pepper
Juice of 1 lemon
1 teaspoon Pernod
1 Idaho potato, cooked and riced or grated
1½ cups olive oil
2 tablespoons chopped fresh basil leaves
2 tablespoons chopped scallions
1 tablespoon chopped fresh cilantro leaves

Place the saffron and water in a small saucepan and bring to a boil over high heat. Turn off the heat and let steep for 10 minutes.

Place the garlic, salt, pepper, cayenne, lemon juice, and Pernod in a blender and process for about 2 minutes, until very smooth and the saffron stamens are finely chopped.

While the machine is running, add the reserved saffron water and the potato. Gradually add the oil in a thin, steady stream and process until smooth. Add the basil, scallions, and cilantro and pulse to combine.

CHICKEN BROTH

Italian Penicillin

$\mathcal{D}$on't overlook the importance of stocks and broths; they are the foundation of good cooking. If you start with a good stock or broth, you will end up with a better, richer-tasting dish. When you make either one, you should want to drink it by itself. Love your stocks and broth and tend to them by skimming away impurities and maintaining an even simmer rather than a boil. Instead of releasing the flavor of the ingredients, boiling locks it in and leaves the broth cloudy and murky.

My grandmother Giuliette used to make a great chicken broth that she fed to me when I was sick. She floated pastene (the tiny star-shaped pasta) in it and grated fresh Parmesan cheese over the top. I still crave it now, sick or well.

At Olives, we make broths and stocks every day, all day long, and I have to admit that we don't always follow recipes religiously. After you've gotten comfortable with the recipe and the idea of making your own, you too will find yourself adding and subtracting your own ingredients. You don't have to add the ham bone, but the enriched flavor of the ham infuses the broth with a great smoky flavor.

MAKES 12 TO 14 CUPS

1 6- to 7-pound chicken, trimmed of excess fat
Carcass and neck of a 6- to 7-pound chicken
1 ham hock or ham bone (optional)
2 celery stalks, chopped
2 carrots, chopped
1 Spanish onion, chopped
2 leeks, chopped
2 garlic cloves

2 bay leaves
1 bunch fresh thyme
1 small bunch fresh oregano
1 teaspoon black peppercorns
1 teaspoon kosher salt, or more to taste
½ teaspoon black pepper, or more to taste

Place the chicken, the chicken carcass, the ham hock, if desired, and the celery, carrots, onion, leeks, garlic, bay leaves, thyme, oregano, and peppercorns in an 8-quart stockpot and cover with cold water. Bring to a boil over high heat. Reduce the heat to low and cook, partially covered, for 3 hours.

Strain the broth, discard the solids, cover, and refrigerate.

When the stock has completely cooled, skim off and discard the hardened fat. Add the salt and pepper.

The broth keeps in the refrigerator for 2 to 3 days and in the freezer for 3 months.

DARK STOCK

$\mathcal{T}$his is a variation on the classic veal stock. Many recipes call for half veal and half beef bones, but I prefer veal, chicken, or pork for the best and lightest flavor. The veal bones create an exquisite stock that tastes meaty, rich, and yet, like veal, delicate. I use a lot of dark stock in my cooking because I like the richness it adds.

You can substitute all chicken bones for the mixed bones and make a dark chicken stock. Never throw bones away: always save them for stock.

MAKES 8 TO 10 CUPS

8 to 10 pounds veal, chicken, or pork bones, or a combination
2 tablespoons olive oil
½ cup tomato paste
2 ham hocks
1 Spanish onion, chopped
4 carrots, chopped
2 leeks, chopped
4 celery stalks, chopped
5 garlic cloves, chopped
1 sprig fresh rosemary
4 cups hearty red wine
1 teaspoon black peppercorns

Preheat the oven to 450 degrees.

Rub the bones with the olive oil and place in a large roasting pan in the oven. Cook until the bones are deeply browned, about 1 hour. Stir the tomato paste into the pan juices and roast for an additional 15 minutes. Add the ham hocks, onion, carrots, leeks, celery, garlic, and rosemary and roast for an additional 45 minutes, stirring every 10 to 15 minutes. Remove the pan from the oven and deglaze with the red wine. Set aside to cool to room temperature.

Transfer the bones and vegetables to a large stockpot, add the black peppercorns, and cover with cold water. Bring to a boil over high heat. Reduce the heat to low and let simmer for at least 6 hours and as long as 12.

Strain the stock and discard the solids. Return the stock to the pot, bring to a boil over medium-high heat, then lower to a simmer and cook until reduced by half. Let cool, stirring occasionally.

At Olives, we use an ice bath that surrounds the stock in order to cool it as quickly as possible. You can simulate this by filling your sink with ice and cold water and placing the stock in it. Cover and refrigerate. The broth keeps in the refrigerator for 2 to 3 days and in the freezer for 3 months.

LOBSTER STOCK

*L*obsters, like many crustaceans, have the most powerful flavor in their shells, rather than in the meat itself. In fact, Chinese and Mexicans grind the shells into a powder that is then used to thicken sauces. It's absolutely critical to use the freshest lobsters you can get, which will yield the stock with the brightest color and best flavor. Lobsters should have a sweet, pure, oceany smell; if not, any off or ammoniated flavor will carry on into the final product.

This stock can be made without the chicken backs, but they mellow and counterbalance the strong taste of the lobster. In addition, the gelatin from the chicken bones enriches and thickens the texture of the stock. Cutting everything into small pieces extracts the maximum flavor.

At Olives we cook many dishes with lobster meat, and although you'll never have a stockpile of lobster bodies as we do, it's worth indulging in the occasional lobster dinner just to make this unusual stock. If you don't have time then, freeze the shells until you do have enough time (or lobsters). Lobster Stock adds immeasurable flavor to dishes like Paella (page 326) and Garlic-Lobster Risotto Calabrese (page 198).

MAKES ABOUT 8 TO 10 CUPS

4 lobster carcasses, chopped

2 to 3 non-oily white fish carcasses (such as sole, halibut, or cod), chopped

2 to 3 chicken backs, chopped

2 cups dry white wine

2 celery stalks, finely chopped

1 carrot, peeled if desired and finely chopped

1 small Spanish onion, finely chopped

1 4-ounce can tomato paste

1 teaspoon dried thyme
2 bay leaves
2 garlic cloves, finely chopped

Place the lobster, fish carcasses, and chicken backs in a large stockpot and cover with cold water. Add the wine, celery, carrot, onion, tomato paste, thyme, bay leaves, and garlic and bring to a simmer over medium-low heat. Simmer gently for 45 minutes.

Strain the stock and discard the solids. Cover and refrigerate. The stock keeps in the refrigerator for 2 to 3 days and in the freezer for 3 months.

CORN STOCK

*T*he nice thing about Corn Stock is that it's a great substitute for a meat or chicken stock in a dish. Obviously, it's particularly good with any dish that has corn in it, such as Toasted Corn Polenta (page 188), Smoky Ham Hock and Corn Risotto (page 196), and Swordfish with Clams, Cilantro, and Corn Broth (page 308), where it adds corn intensity. It's also wonderful for poaching fish and chicken.

- *Stockpile your corncobs. Some of the greatest flavor of corn is in the cob. By cooking them this way, you extract their intense flavor.*

- *Never buy corn that has already been husked. Instead buy unshucked ears with fresh-looking, pale-yellow, dry silk.*

MAKES ABOUT 10 TO 12 CUPS

1 leek, well washed, chopped
4 celery stalks, chopped
16 corncobs (corn kernels removed and reserved for another dish)
6 garlic cloves, coarsely chopped
1 large bunch fresh thyme
1 bay leaf
½ teaspoon black peppercorns
About 16 cups cold water

Place the leek, celery, corncobs, garlic, thyme, bay leaf, and peppercorns in a large stockpot and cover with cold water. Bring to a boil over high heat. Reduce the heat to low and simmer, uncovered, for 2 hours.

Strain the stock and discard the solids. Cover and refrigerate. The broth keeps in the refrigerator for 2 to 3 days and in the freezer for 3 months.

■ *CORN TALK*

Native to North America, corn has a rich and diverse history. It was first cultivated and harvested by Native Americans and has since crossed many oceans, but I know of no other culture that uses it more than our own, whether as part of a summer barbecue, or in Jasper White's Corn and Lobster Chowder, or. . . . Think about it, you probably eat corn every day: corn syrup, cornstarch, cornmeal, cornflakes, the list goes on.

Sweet corn stock is best made in the mid- to late summer or early fall, depending upon where you live. In New England, where we tend to be very picky about our corn, the first fresh corn shows up in July, but the best comes a little later, when the native sweet, white Silver Queen corn arrives. I love going to roadstands in the late afternoon and watching people pick through the corn to be sure the kernels are plump and full. Once the ears are harvested, the sugar in the corn breaks down very easily and turns to starch, so it's best eaten within a few hours. There are many types of corn grown for many different reasons, but I challenge anyone to show me anything better than that grown in New England. There is something about the soil and the climate that makes it so special. At the time of year when corn is at its peak, the menu at Olives becomes packed with corn specials, including Tomato and Corn Salad (page 124), fish, clams, and lobster steamed in corn stock, or, my favorite, simple, sweet, delicious creamed corn: I love to toss creamed corn onto pappardelle noodles with a little butter and Parmesan cheese.

I hate frozen corn. I do, however, love creamed corn in a can, no doubt a throwback to my Southern upbringing.

BLACK OLIVE PASTE

*I*n any of the recipes calling for olive paste, you can use store-bought, but we prefer to make our own, so that we can be sure of getting exactly what we want. This is great spread on crostini, used as a dip, or mixed into spaghetti as in Chilled Black Olive Spaghetti Salad (page 212).

MAKES ABOUT 1¼ CUPS

1 cup pitted black olives, such as Kalamata, oil-cured, or Gaeta
5 anchovy fillets
5 garlic cloves
¾ cup virgin olive oil
1 tablespoon fresh rosemary leaves or 1 teaspoon dried rosemary
1 teaspoon kosher salt
½ teaspoon black pepper

Place the olives, anchovy fillets, garlic, olive oil, rosemary, salt, and pepper in a blender or food processor fitted with a steel blade and blend into a smooth paste.

WALNUT ROMESCO

*T*his is a play on the traditional Catalonian romesco sauce, which uses almonds. Try it on Stuffed Zucchini Pancakes (page 158), Fig Polenta (page 182), or grilled fish, beef, or chicken—or mix it with a can of white tuna for lunch.

■ *Nuts should be purchased whole and stored in a cool, dry place for no longer than three months and in the refrigerator for no more than six.*

MAKES ABOUT 2 CUPS

1 cup plus 1 teaspoon olive oil
2 garlic cloves, thinly sliced
½ cup walnuts
¼ small white onion, thinly sliced
2 plum tomatoes, fresh or canned, sliced
1 roasted red bell pepper (see page 48) (optional)
¼ teaspoon crushed red pepper flakes
1 ancho chile, stemmed and chopped (optional)
1 tablespoon sherry vinegar
Juice of ½ lemon
¼ cup fresh bread crumbs
½ cup extra-virgin olive oil
1 teaspoon kosher salt
¼ teaspoon black pepper

Place a medium-size skillet over medium-high heat and when it is hot, add the 1 teaspoon olive oil. Add the garlic and cook for 2 minutes. Add the walnuts, onion, tomatoes, roasted pepper, red pepper flakes, and ancho chile, stirring well after each addition, and cook until the nuts are lightly toasted, about 2 minutes. Transfer to a blender, add the sherry vinegar and lemon juice, and process until it forms a chunky paste. Add the bread crumbs and pulse. While the machine is running, gradually add the remaining 1 cup olive oil and the ½ cup extra-virgin olive oil in a thin, steady stream. Add the salt and pepper and process to blend.

Walnut Romesco keeps for 2 to 3 days in the refrigerator.

ROASTED BELL PEPPERS

Sweet bell peppers are one of the most misused vegetables. They are used too often to add color to a dish, with no thought given as to whether or not they add the right flavor.

■ *Sweet bell peppers should be brightly colored, with no soft or discolored spots. They can be refrigerated up to one week.*

MAKES 6 PEPPERS

6 yellow, orange, purple, or red bell peppers

Prepare the grill or preheat the broiler.

Place the peppers directly on the grill or on a pan broiler about 2 inches away from the heat source and roast, turning, until they are singed on all sides, about 10 minutes.

Transfer the peppers to a deep bowl or container and cover with plastic wrap. When they are cool enough to handle, run them under cold water, peel off the charred skin, and remove the seeds. Use immediately or store in the refrigerator for no more than 1 week.

STARTERS ▪

OLIVES OLIVES

Olives, God's gift to the Mediterranean (and for me the very definition), were the inspiration for our restaurant, which is based on the cuisine of the sun-drenched Mediterranean. Olives grow in arid places where almost nothing else grows—it has been said that they take so little, yet give back so much. The trees are beautiful—subtle pastel colors, silvery leaves—even Van Gogh couldn't get enough of them.

These marinated olives have graced each table from the very first day Olives opened. They're the perfect appetizer, awakening your appetite without sating it. Although olive purists might disagree with me, the real fun of this dish is to use olives of all different sizes, textures, and flavors.

This recipe makes a large batch, but since the olives store so well, it's worth making the whole amount to have some around. They can turn a simple dinner into something more special.

■ *The olives we use at Olives are the meaty ones. Some of my favorites include:*

Gaeta—small wrinkled black Italian olives with a salty, plum-y taste.

Kalamata—smooth medium-sized black olives with a fruity taste.

Oil-cured black—small jet-black olives with a smoky flavor. I use them when I want a rich, salty, slightly bitter taste.

Bella di Cerignola—huge green southern Italian olives that are somewhat like avocados in texture.

MAKES ABOUT 4 CUPS

MARINADE:
Grated zest of ½ orange
Grated zest of ½ lemon
2 garlic cloves, minced
¼ cup chopped fresh flat-leaf parsley leaves
1 to 2 tablespoons chopped fresh rosemary leaves or 1 to 2 teaspoons
*   dried rosemary*
2 teaspoons chopped fresh oregano leaves or heaping ½ teaspoon
*   dried oregano*
1 teaspoon chopped peeled fresh ginger
½ teaspoon fennel seeds
¼ to ½ teaspoon crushed red pepper flakes
1 teaspoon kosher salt
1 teaspoon black pepper

4 cups assorted olives, such as Niçoise, Kalamata, Picholine, Alphonso,
*   and/or Sicilian green*
Virgin olive oil, to cover

To make the marinade: Place the orange zest, lemon zest, garlic, parsley, rosemary, oregano, ginger, fennel, pepper flakes, salt, and pepper in a food processor fitted with a steel blade and pulse until the mixture forms a chunky paste.

Toss the olives with the marinade and cover with the olive oil. Serve immediately, or place in a glass jar and let marinate at room temperature for up to 1 month or refrigerate for up to 3 months.

Deep-Fried Green Olives Stuffed with Sausage and Goat Cheese

*A*s a rule, I don't like making small individual hors d'oeuvres, because you spend so much time for so little result. I do, however, make an exception for these, because they taste incredible. Briny tart green olives stuffed with sausage is a great classic flavor combination and the goat cheese enriches it even more, taking its flavor from the homey to the sublime.

SERVES 9 TO 12; MAKES 36

STUFFING:
2 teaspoons olive oil
2 garlic cloves, minced
1 small white onion, finely diced
1 pound sweet or spicy Italian sausage, removed from casings and
  crumbled as you cook it
1 cup crumbled goat cheese
1 tablespoon chopped fresh flat-leaf parsley leaves
1 teaspoon finely chopped fresh oregano leaves or scant ½ teaspoon
  dried oregano
1 cup fresh bread crumbs

36 large brine-cured green olives, such as Sicilian or colossal,
  halved and pitted
1 cup all-purpose flour
3 large eggs, beaten
½ cup fresh bread crumbs
2 cups olive oil, for deep-frying

To make the stuffing: Place a large skillet over medium heat and when it is hot add the oil. Add the garlic, onion, and sausage, stirring well after each addition, and cook until the sausage has browned, about 5 minutes. Off the heat, add the goat cheese, parsley, oregano, and the 1 cup bread crumbs and stir well. Set aside to cool.

Place 1 teaspoon of the stuffing in each of half of the olive halves. Place the remaining olive halves on top and press together.

Place the flour, eggs, and the ½ cup bread crumbs in three separate bowls. Roll the olives in the flour, then in the eggs, and then in the bread crumbs.

To deep-fry the olives: Reheat the skillet over medium-high heat and add the olive oil. When the oil is hot, gently drop in the olives, in batches, and cook until the breading is lightly browned, about 1 to 2 minutes. Gently transfer to a paper towel and blot dry. Repeat until all the olives have been fried. Serve immediately.

OLIVES CRAB CAKES

*C*rabmeat is one of the most underrated tastes and textures to come out of the water. Delicate, interesting, and elegant—I love it even more than lobster. When I can resist eating all the crabmeat straight out of the container, my favorite preparation is crab cakes, particularly in the spring and early summer, when the Jonah crabs first come out of Maine's icy waters. When you cut into these, you should see big, tender, sweet, succulent pieces of crabmeat.

Serve them either on a bed of simple greens, drizzled with Spicy Aïoli (page 35) or Citrus Aïoli (page 36), or on any of these salads: Crab and Cucumber Slaw (page 118), Shaved Raw Fennel and Red Onion Salad (page 121), Tomato and Corn Salad (page 124), or Arugula Salad with Tomato and Cucumber Juice (page 125).

In the winter months, try them with something heartier, like the Toasted Corn Polenta (page 188), or the Country Walnut Mashed Potatoes (page 174) or Chorizo Mashed Potatoes (page 172).

■ *My rules of thumb about using crabmeat are to never overcook or overmix it, to leave it in its most natural state, and not to mask its delicate and sweet flavor with overpowering sauces or ingredients (e.g., mornay sauce or bell peppers).*

SERVES 4 AS AN APPETIZER OR 2 FOR LUNCH

½ pound crabmeat, preferably Jonah crab or rock, pulled apart but not shredded, picked over for shells
2 tablespoons sour cream or yogurt
1 heaping tablespoon Dijon mustard
2 tablespoons finely chopped scallion (white part only)
1 tablespoon minced fresh chervil or parsley leaves

1 large egg, lightly beaten
1 teaspoon kosher salt
½ teaspoon black pepper
6 tablespoons fresh bread crumbs
¼ cup all-purpose flour
2 tablespoons olive oil

Place the crabmeat, sour cream, mustard, scallions, chervil, egg, salt, pepper, and bread crumbs in a large bowl and toss lightly to combine. Do not overmix.

Place the flour on a large plate. Divide the crab mixture into 4 patties and dredge in the flour.

Place a large skillet over medium-high heat and when it is hot, add the oil. Gently place the patties in the skillet and cook until they are golden brown, about 5 minutes on each side. Serve immediately.

FOCACCIA

Almost every cuisine and culture has a flatbread as one of its dietary staples. Greeks have pita bread, Israelis have matzo, and Italians have focaccia, one of my favorites. Focaccia is a simple leavened flat bread that is extremely versatile; it can be served as part of a starter, a whole meal, or a side dish, or used in a sandwich. Flavorful and sexy when served warm, it should have a crust that crackles and a soft, creamy texture inside. My favorite way to eat it is fresh from the oven, slathered with extra-virgin olive oil and sprinkled with Parmesan cheese.

Just in case my favorite way isn't yours, here are three alternatives. Feel free to improvise and indulge your own ideas.

> ■ *Fresh Parmesan cheese should be grated or shaved right at the table, where it will lend enormous flavor and quality to whatever you're serving. The best is Parmigiano-Reggiano. Made from cow's milk and aged about two years, it should be smooth, creamy, and a little nutty and salty. We also use, and often substitute, Pecorino Romano, which is made from sheep's milk, aged about one year, and a little sharper than Parmigiano.*

MAKES 4 FOCACCIAS

DOUGH:
¼ cup whole-wheat flour
3½ cups all-purpose flour
2 teaspoons (¼ ounce) fresh compressed, crumbled yeast
2 teaspoons kosher salt
2 teaspoons white sugar

2 teaspoons extra-virgin olive oil

1⅔ cups lukewarm water, 98 to 100°

TOPPING 1:

1 tablespoon extra-virgin olive oil

½ teaspoon kosher salt

¼ cup grated Parmesan cheese

TOPPING 2:

1 tablespoon extra-virgin olive oil

½ teaspoon kosher salt

2 roasted Vidalia onions (see page 30)

4 plum tomatoes, fresh or canned, thinly sliced

12 fresh basil leaves

¼ cup grated Parmesan cheese

¼ cup shaved aged provolone cheese

TOPPING 3:

1 tablespoon extra-virgin olive oil

½ teaspoon kosher salt

6 to 8 fresh figs, quartered

2 tablespoons honey

1 tablespoon roughly chopped fresh rosemary leaves or 1 teaspoon
*   dried rosemary*

8 thin slices prosciutto

To make the dough: Combine the flours, yeast, salt, and sugar in the bowl of a mixer fitted with a dough hook. While the mixer is running, gradually add the oil and water. Knead on low speed until the dough is firm and smooth, about 10 minutes.

Divide the dough into 4 balls (about 7½ ounces each). Let them rise in a warm spot, covered with a damp towel, until doubled in bulk, about 1 to 2 hours.

Preheat the oven to 400 degrees. Place a baking stone in the oven.

To prepare the focaccia: Place each ball of dough on a lightly floured surface and punch down with your fingertips into a 7- to 8-inch disk, so that you end up with a dimpled surface. Drizzle the surfaces with the oil and then evenly distribute the remaining ingredients—except the prosciutto for Topping #3, which you add after the focaccia has been baked.

Place the focaccias on a baking stone in the oven and bake until golden brown, about 15 to 20 minutes.

August Tomato Tart

*T*his dish is a showcase for the meaty, juicy, sweet beefsteak. I call this August Tomato Tart because it should be made only when beefsteak tomatoes are at their peak, in August and September.

For a light lunch, serve this with a mixed green salad with Shallot Vinaigrette (page 33) or Artichoke Guacamole (page 92) and a cold glass of Sauvignon Blanc: its grassy, acidic flavor will complement the flavors perfectly.

SERVES 4 AS AN APPETIZER OR 2 FOR LUNCH

1 recipe Tart Dough (page 60)
½ cup chopped slab bacon or chopped high-quality thick-sliced lean bacon
  (or substitute 1 tablespoon olive oil)
1 tablespoon chopped fresh rosemary leaves or 1 teaspoon dried rosemary
1 red onion, halved and thinly sliced
3 garlic cloves, thinly sliced
1 to 2 ripe red or yellow beefsteak tomatoes, sliced into about 6 even slices
¼ cup crumbled feta or goat cheese
¼ cup chopped fresh basil leaves
1 tablespoon chopped fresh mint leaves
½ teaspoon kosher salt
¼ teaspoon black pepper

Preheat the oven to 375 degrees.

Roll out the tart dough on a floured surface into a 10-inch round. Fit the dough into an 8-inch cast-iron skillet and crimp the edges.

Place a skillet over medium-high heat and when it is hot, add the bacon. Cook until it begins to render its fat, about 4 minutes. Add the rosemary and cook until the bacon is crispy but not browned, about 1 minute. Drain the bacon on paper towels. Pour off all but 1 tablespoon of the bacon fat.

Reheat the skillet, and add the onion and garlic. Cook until the onion is golden and soft, about 8 minutes.

Spread the onion mixture evenly on the prepared dough and add the tomatoes, arranging them in an overlapping circle. Sprinkle with the reserved bacon, feta, basil, mint, salt, and black pepper.

Bake the tart for 10 to 12 minutes.

TART DOUGH

*A*t Olives, we use a much more complicated, time-consuming dough than this one for our tarts; it's essentially our pizza dough with butter folded in. This dough is simple and takes little time.

MAKES ONE 9- TO 10-INCH TART

1⅛ cups all purpose flour
1½ teaspoons white sugar
¼ teaspoon kosher salt
¼ cup cold water
8 tablespoons unsalted butter, cold, cut into 8 to 10 pieces

Place the flour, sugar, and salt in the bowl of a food processor fitted with a steel blade and pulse to combine. Add the water and pulse again. While the machine is running, add the butter pieces, one at a time, pulsing well between additions and pulsing until the dough just begins to come together. Form into a ball, cover with plastic wrap, and refrigerate for about 20 minutes.

BLACK OLIVE TOASTS

*W*hen I think about the deep, earthy flavors of the Mediterranean, these are the ingredients that come to mind: olives, anchovies, garlic, and rosemary.

Serve these finger sandwiches with Marinated Roasted Red Peppers (page 117). Don't be tempted to eat a whole uncut sandwich; these are far too rich. And don't substitute processed mozzarella for the fresh; if you can't find fresh mozzarella, use an equal amount of ricotta.

> ■ *The best ricotta cheese can be found freshly made in specialty cheese and Italian food stores. Ricotta is made from whey, and is light, creamy, and delicate. Although fresh ricotta tends to be less watery than packaged, if you are using it instead of mozzarella in this recipe, it is fine to use the packaged. If you use packaged, drain it in a muslin- or cheesecloth-lined strainer for about 30 minutes to thicken it.*

SERVES 8 TO 10

5 to 6 tablespoons Black Olive Paste (page 46) or store-bought
*   (San Remo brand is good)*
10 thin slices dense, hearty country bread
8 to 10 ounces fresh mozzarella cheese, sliced
1 to 2 tablespoons olive oil

Spread about 1 tablespoon of the olive paste on each of five bread slices, top with the mozzarella, and then top with the remaining slices of bread.

Place a large nonstick skillet over medium-high heat and when it is hot, add the oil. Place the sandwiches in the pan and cook until the cheese has melted and both sides are golden brown, about 2 minutes per side. Cut into small sandwiches.

TUNA TARTARE

$\mathcal{I}$'m a sushi freak! And tuna is one of my favorites. I love discovering the different cultures that eat raw and marinated fish, and when I went to Italy I was very surprised to see that it was one of them. The Japanese are the most obvious, but I think about eating oysters and littlenecks on the half-shell in New England, conch seviche in the Bahamas, and all the ceviches of South and Central America. It is important to preserve these traditions, but the only way to accomplish that is to ensure safe and clean waters which will, in turn, ensure a consistent, safe, and fresh supply of fish.

At Olives, we used to serve Tuna Tartare with Fried Oysters (page 64), until a customer came in and wanted the tuna but didn't eat shellfish. So we started serving it with Carl's Pagoda-Inspired Tomato Soup (page 111) and discovered we liked the combination even better. The tuna is also great served on cucumber slices or toast points.

Before you make this dish, be sure you have a good relationship with a reputable fishmonger and let him know that you will be serving the fish raw. Ask for yellowfin or bluefin tuna, and accept only tuna with a vibrant, garnet-red color, a firm texture, and absolutely no odor. Remember that raw fish is very rich, so serve small amounts.

This makes a great starter for Roasted Clams with Chicken, Tomatoes, Artichokes, and Bacon (page 314) or Steamed Tagine of Halibut with Moroccan-Spiced Spaghetti Squash (page 324).

SERVES 8

*1½ pounds very fresh bluefin or yellowfin tuna, diced into pieces the size
    of a raisin
1 tablespoon chopped fresh basil leaves
1 tablespoon chopped fresh cilantro leaves
1 tablespoon finely chopped peeled fresh ginger
Greens from 1 bunch scallions, finely chopped*

½ to 1 teaspoon Vietnamese chili paste (see Note)

2 teaspoons soy sauce

½ teaspoon black pepper

1 to 2 teaspoons kosher salt

2 tablespoons extra-virgin olive oil

1 teaspoon toasted sesame oil

Combine all the ingredients in a large bowl. Cover and chill for no longer than 1 hour before serving.

> NOTE: *If you cannot find Vietnamese chili paste, you can substitute Chinese or Thai chili paste, which you should be able to find in any well-stocked grocery store. Because different brands vary in degrees of hotness, we suggest that you add a small amount at a time and taste after each addition.*

FRIED OYSTERS

When I was a child, my family took vacations to Savannah and Jekyll Island, where one of our first stops was always at a roadside fish joint specializing in fried oysters. Those were the days when I didn't know or care what cholesterol was.

One of the greatest and most sinfully delicious things in life is a great fried oyster. When you're looking for elegance; serve these with Tuna Tartare (page 62). And when you're not, make Oyster Po' Boys and serve four to six oysters each on hoagie rolls with Spicy Aïoli (page 35), iceberg lettuce, sliced pickles, and sliced red onions. The oysters can also be served mounded on top of grilled fillet of beef "carpetbagger's style" or on Shaved Raw Fennel and Red Onion Salad (page 121) or Roquefort Caesar Salad (page 126), minus the Roquefort.

■ *Unless you know your fishmonger and are sure that the oysters are from a reliable source, don't buy oysters preshucked.*

SERVES 6 TO 8

1 cup buttermilk
2 large eggs, beaten
3 tablespoons chopped fresh mint leaves
¼ cup fresh bread crumbs or 3 tablespoons all-purpose flour and
*   1 tablespoon stone-ground yellow cornmeal*
½ cup olive oil
24 oysters, freshly shucked (see above)

Beat the buttermilk, eggs, and mint together in a small bowl.
Place the bread crumbs in another small bowl.

Place a large skillet over medium-high heat and when it is hot, add the oil. When the oil is very hot, dip the oysters, a few at a time, in the egg mixture and then in the bread crumbs and gently place in the oil. Fry the oysters in batches, making sure the oil is hot prior to each addition, until they are golden brown, about 1½ minutes per side. Drain well on paper towels. Serve immediately.

ARTICHOKE PANCAKES WITH GOAT CHEESE

I stumbled upon this savory pancake when trying to come up with a new vegetarian dish. I made an artichoke puree to use as a sauce but it came out too thick, and it looked just like my typical pancake batter. So I decided to cook it like pancakes and discovered an amazingly sexy, silky texture and rich artichoke flavor.

These make a great accompaniment to Portobello Piccata (page 160). For a heartier meal, pair them with Mountain Lamb Scaloppine with Figs and Honey (page 274), Osso Buco of Veal (page 264), Garlic-Studded Rack of Veal (page 263), or Grilled Marinated Tuna (page 288). Serve with glasses of ice-cold beer; artichokes and wine do not go together.

Although it seems like a lot of work, it's worth taking the time to use fresh artichokes.

■ *When buying fresh artichokes, look for small artichokes with deep green color and a heavy weight. Avoid any that are browned, shriveled, or feel hollow.*

SERVES 4: MAKES 8 LITTLE OR 4 LARGE PANCAKES

3 fresh, frozen, or canned artichoke bottoms
2 lemons, cut in half
3 large eggs
¼ cup water
⅓ cup all-purpose flour
1 teaspoon kosher salt
½ teaspoon black pepper
2 large egg whites
1 tablespoon olive oil

3 tablespoons crumbled goat cheese
1 tablespoon sour cream

Fill a large bowl with ice water.
If using fresh artichokes, prepare as follows:

- *To prepare artichoke bottoms, slice off the stems of the artichokes and remove any tough outer leaves. Place them in a large nonaluminum pot and cover them with cold water. Squeeze the lemons into the pot, add the juice and the lemon halves to the pot, and bring to a boil over high heat. Reduce the heat to medium and cook until the artichokes are tender, about 25 minutes. Use the tines of a fork to check for tenderness.*

  Place the artichokes in the ice water. When they are cool enough to handle, drain and remove the leaves and the fuzzy chokes. Trim off the edges of the bottoms.

Preheat the oven to 350 degrees.

Place the artichoke bottoms, eggs, and water in a blender or a food processor fitted with a steel blade and blend until creamy. Pour into a mixing bowl, add the flour, salt, and pepper, and combine until the mixture forms a thick paste.

Whip the egg whites in a dry copper or stainless steel bowl until they hold stiff peaks. Gently fold into the artichoke mixture.

Place a cast-iron skillet over medium-high heat and when it is hot, add the oil. Drop dollops of batter (about 2 tablespoons per pancake), a few at a time, into the hot oil. When the edges begin to stiffen, turn the pancakes over and cook until lightly golden, about 2 minutes. Place the pancakes on an ovenproof plate.

Combine the goat cheese and sour cream in a small mixing bowl. Top each pancake with a large dollop of the goat cheese mixture and place in the oven until the cheese just begins to melt, about 2 minutes.

CORN CAKES WITH WHIPPED GOAT CHEESE

*M*ake this in the summer when corn is at its peak and you'll get a nice intense flavor. Slice the kernels off the cob right over the mixing bowl so you'll be sure to get the milk that comes out of the corn. (It may be tempting to use canned or frozen corn for a dish like this one, but please don't.)

Although this is a great starter for dinner, it also is one of my favorite brunch dishes, simply served with a salad. For a once-a-year dinner, serve it with BBQ Slow-Roasted Suckling Pig with Ginger-Honey Glaze (page 270).

SERVES 4 TO 6; MAKES 12 PANCAKES

PANCAKES:
3 large eggs
2½ cups fresh corn kernels
½ cup stone-ground yellow cornmeal
1 teaspoon kosher salt
½ teaspoon black pepper
½ cup chopped scallions
3 large egg whites

WHIPPED GOAT CHEESE:
1 cup crumbled soft goat cheese
3 tablespoons sour cream
2 teaspoons finely chopped fresh rosemary leaves or ⅔ teaspoon
*   dried rosemary*
½ teaspoon kosher salt
¼ teaspoon black pepper

2 teaspoons olive oil

To make the pancakes: Place the eggs and 1½ cups of the corn in a blender or a food processor fitted with a steel blade and mix until smooth. Place the corn mixture in a mixing bowl and add the cornmeal, salt, pepper, scallions, and the remaining 1 cup corn.

Whip the egg whites in a dry copper or stainless steel bowl until they hold stiff peaks. Fold into the corn mixture.

Preheat the oven to 350 degrees.

To make the whipped goat cheese: Place the goat cheese, sour cream, rosemary, salt, and pepper in a small mixing bowl and combine well.

Place a large skillet over medium heat and when it is hot, add the oil. Drop quarter-cupfuls of the pancake batter, a few at a time, into the hot skillet and cook until the pancakes are golden brown, about 2 minutes per side. Place the pancakes on a baking sheet as they are finished.

Place a large dollop of the goat cheese on each pancake and place in the oven until the cheese just begins to melt, about 2 minutes.

OLIVES TART

I designed this, which is somewhat like the classic French onion tart pissaladière, to be a signature item featuring all the wonderful lusty flavors of the Mediterranean. It hasn't been off the menu since the day we opened.

If you happen to have a brick oven, your tart will come out just like ours, baked the old-fashioned way. But if you don't, don't worry. Bake it in a traditional oven. Either way, it' s a great starter, filled with complexity and richness.

When you're making this, keep in mind that it is a delicate tart rather than anything quiche-like, with a few ingredients thinly placed over the tart pastry. It makes a great lunch paired with a mixed green salad.

■ *Canned anchovies should be stored in the refrigerator after they've been opened. If your anchovies have been packed in salt, be sure to rinse and dry them before using. If your anchovies are packed in a tin, transfer any leftovers to a small glass jar.*

SERVES 6 AS AN APPETIZER OR 4 FOR LUNCH

1 tablespoon unsalted butter
½ Spanish onion, thinly sliced
4 tablespoons Black Olive Paste (page 46) or store-bought
*   (San Remo brand is good)*
1 recipe Tart Dough (page 60)
⅓ to ½ cup assorted cured black and green olives, pitted and roughly chopped
¼ cup crumbled goat cheese
1 to 2 anchovy fillets, roughly chopped
1 large fresh rosemary sprig, leaves only, plus 2 whole sprigs, for garnish

Preheat the oven to 450 degrees.
Place a large cast-iron skillet over medium heat and melt the butter.

Add the onions and cook until they are soft and golden, about 10 to 12 minutes. Set aside to cool.

Roll out the tart dough on a floured surface into a 10-inch round. Fit the dough into a 9-inch tart pan.

Spread the olive paste evenly over the bottom of the tart shell. Add the onions in an even layer, then scatter the chopped olives, goat cheese, anchovies, and rosemary leaves over the top.

Place in the oven and bake for 20 to 25 minutes, or until the crust is a crispy golden brown and the goat cheese has browned a little.

Serve at room temperature, garnished with the rosemary sprigs.

Napoleon of Seared Foie Gras and Artichoke Crisps with Artichoke Mash and Shallot-Honey Glaze

*E*ating foie gras is one of the truly great gastronomic experiences. Michael Ginor, one of my closest friends, and his partner, Izzy Yanay, are the owners of Hudson Valley Foie Gras, in Ferndale, New York, which is among the largest and best producers of foie gras in the world. In 1993, Michael arranged a promotional tour to The Shangri La Hotel in Hong Kong, where we cooked this sweet, comforting, and decadent dish every day for ten days. Needless to say, it was quite a hit.

SERVES 6

SHALLOT-HONEY GLAZE:
1 tablespoon unsalted butter
3 shallots, thinly sliced
2 tablespoons honey or lightly packed brown sugar
¼ cup balsamic vinegar
3 tablespoons orange juice
1 cup Dark Stock (page 40) or Chicken Broth (page 38)

ARTICHOKE CRISPS:
¼ cup all-purpose flour
4 fresh artichoke bottoms (see instructions on page 67), cut into 12 slices
1 tablespoon olive oil

SEARED FOIE GRAS:
1 pound raw foie gras, cut into 12 slices ½ inch thick and about 3 inches
    long (available at specialty food shops or by mail order, see page 351)

1 teaspoon kosher salt
½ teaspoon black pepper

ARTICHOKE MASH:
1 Idaho potato, peeled and cubed
1 cup chopped artichoke bottoms, fresh, canned, or frozen
1 garlic clove, minced
1 tablespoon fresh rosemary leaves
½ teaspoon kosher salt

To make the shallot-honey glaze: Place a small saucepan over medium-high heat and add the butter. Add the shallots and cook until they are golden, about 5 minutes. Add the honey or sugar, balsamic vinegar, and orange juice and simmer until the mixture is reduced, bubbly, and syrupy, about 5 minutes. Add the stock and cook until it is bubbly and syrupy, about 3 to 5 minutes. Remove from the heat.

To make the artichoke crisps: Spread the flour on a plate and dredge the artichoke slices in the flour. Place a small skillet over medium-high heat and when it is hot, add the oil. Add the artichokes and cook in batches until they are browned and crispy, about 3 minutes. Transfer to a plate.

To cook the foie gras: Reheat the pan. Sprinkle the foie gras with the 1 teaspoon salt and the ½ teaspoon pepper, add it to the pan and cook until it is a deep golden brown, about 1½ to 2½ minutes. Baste with the rendered fat.

To make the artichoke mash: Place the potato, artichoke bottoms, garlic, and rosemary and the ½ teaspoon salt in a medium pot and cover with water. Bring to a boil over medium-high heat and cook until the potato is tender, about 10 to 12 minutes. Drain, place in a bowl, and mash with a fork.

To assemble the napoleons: Place an artichoke crisp in the center of each plate and fill with about 2 tablespoons of the artichoke mash and a slice of foie gras. Place another artichoke crisp on top and fill with artichoke mash and foie gras. Top with another artichoke crisp. Spoon the glaze over the top.

LOBSTER COCKTAIL WITH YELLOW TOMATO AND HORSERADISH VINAIGRETTE

*T*his is an adaptation and refinement of shrimp cocktail. I've substituted lobster for the shrimp and jazzed up the basic chili catsup. As much as I may knock bad wedding food, I'm always relieved when there's a big bowl of shrimp cocktail. The fresh snap of the shrimp combined with the sweet and peppery twang of the sauce are the reasons you'll find me perched at the bowl. You can certainly make this with fresh shrimp, but the lobster adds a real elegance.

■ *Most people aren't accustomed to using fresh horseradish, but once you do, you'll see that there's really no comparison between the bottle and the real thing. Once grated, horseradish loses its pungency very quickly, so you'll taste the difference immediately. When using fresh horseradish, peel off the skin and then either use a hand grater or a food processor. And be careful—horseradish has the same effect on some people as onions, so watch for tears.*

SERVES 4 TO 6

YELLOW TOMATO AND HORSERADISH VINAIGRETTE:
3 ripe yellow (or red) beefsteak tomatoes
¼ cup virgin olive oil
3 garlic cloves, finely chopped
2 tablespoons fresh lemon juice (about ½ lemon)
1 teaspoon sherry vinegar
1 cup finely grated fresh horseradish (do not substitute jarred)

¼ cup chopped fresh cilantro leaves
2 scallions, chopped
1 teaspoon kosher salt
½ teaspoon black pepper

1 pound cooked lobster meat (or meat from three 1-pound lobsters)
Mixed lettuces for serving

To make the vinaigrette: Bring a large pot of water to a boil over high heat. Add the tomatoes and let the water return to a boil. Cook for 3 to 4 minutes, drain, and set aside. When the tomatoes are cool enough to handle, peel off the skins, seed the tomatoes, and roughly chop the flesh.

Place a large skillet over medium-high heat and when it is hot, add the oil. Add the garlic and tomatoes and cook for 1 minute, or until the tomatoes are wilted. Transfer to a medium-size bowl.

Add the lemon juice, vinegar, horseradish, cilantro, scallions, salt, and pepper. Chill for at least 1 hour or up to 24 hours.

Just prior to serving, stir in the lobster. Serve immediately on a bed of greens.

NOTES: *The yellow tomato and horseradish vinaigrette is also great on grilled steak or any kind of fish or seafood, especially oysters. If you start with whole lobsters, remember to save the bodies to make Lobster Stock (page 42).*

RICOTTA MOZZARELLA IN CARROZZA WITH TOMATOES AND OLIVES

*T*he classic Italian dish Ricotta Mozzarella in Carrozza ("cheese in a carriage") is really a fancy name for a grilled cheese sandwich—but it shows how innovative Italians are with their use of bread. At Olives, we bread it instead of putting it between two slices of bread. The combination of sweet ricotta, mozzarella, and tomatoes is a Neapolitan favorite. (Do not try this with processed mozzarella.)

SERVES 6

SAUCE:
¼ cup virgin olive oil
5 garlic cloves, thinly sliced
1 anchovy fillet, chopped
*3 fresh beefsteak tomatoes or 8 to 10 canned plum tomatoes, cut
     into small dice*
½ cup water
1 tablespoon balsamic vinegar
1 teaspoon kosher salt
1 teaspoon black pepper
Greens from 1 bunch scallions, chopped
1 small bunch fresh basil leaves, roughly chopped

CARROZZE:
3 cups ricotta cheese
*2 tablespoons Black Olive Paste (page 46) or store-bought
     (San Remo brand is good)*
1½ cups coarse dry bread crumbs

3 tablespoons chopped fresh oregano or basil leaves
1 teaspoon kosher salt
½ teaspoon black pepper
8 ounces fresh buffalo or cow's milk mozzarella cheese, diced

1 cup all-purpose flour
2 large eggs, beaten
2 cups olive oil, for deep-frying

To make the sauce: Place a large skillet over medium-high heat and when it is hot, add the oil. Add the garlic and cook until it is golden and lightly toasted, about 2 to 3 minutes. Add the anchovy and tomatoes and cook for 5 minutes, stirring occasionally. Add the water, balsamic vinegar, salt, pepper, scallion greens, and basil and simmer for about 2 minutes.

Combine the ricotta cheese, the olive paste, ½ cup of the bread crumbs, the oregano, salt, and pepper in a medium-size mixing bowl. Stir in the mozzarella. Divide into 6 cakes.

Place the flour, eggs, and the remaining 1 cup bread crumbs in three separate shallow bowls. Dip the *carrozze* into the flour, then into the eggs, and then into the bread crumbs. Lightly shape each one into a biscuit-like form.

Place the oil in a large skillet and heat it over medium-high heat until it is very hot but not smoking. Add the *carrozze,* a few at a time, being careful not to crowd the pan, and deep-fry until golden, about 5 to 6 minutes per side. (This will take about two or three batches.) Drain on paper towels and set aside.

Spoon the sauce onto a large serving plate and top with the *carrozze.* Serve immediately. (These should be served hot and cannot be reheated.)

GARLIC SCAMPI AND PAN-FRIED CORNMEAL-CRUSTED BEEFSTEAK TOMATOES

*S*eeing "Shrimp Scampi" on a menu is one of my pet peeves. When I first started cooking, I didn't know that *scampi* actually means shrimp, but now that I do, it drives me crazy to see a description that means nothing. Don't get me wrong, I love the flavor combination—just do me a favor and ask for Garlic Scampi the next time you see "Shrimp Scampi" on a menu.

Here is my version of the classic dish garlic scampi. The crispness of the cornmeal crust and the acidity and sweetness of the tomato cut the richness of the olive oil, all in all making this garlic-and-shrimp combo one of the greatest.

> ■ *As a rule, I slice garlic cloves, because then your dish is infused with a nice toasty garlic flavor without the harshness you sometimes get from chopped garlic. However, it's useful to know that the strength of the flavor depends on the amount of oil released— which is why roasted garlic is so mild and crushed is the most pungent. Vary the way you prepare garlic depending on the strength desired. Elephant garlic is the mildest of all, so don't substitute it for regular garlic.*

SERVES 4 AS AN APPETIZER OR 2 AS AN ENTRÉE

2 large eggs, lightly beaten
¼ cup stone-ground yellow cornmeal
3 beefsteak tomatoes, cut into 1-inch slices
1 teaspoon kosher salt
½ teaspoon black pepper

¼ cup olive oil

½ red onion, thinly sliced

2 tablespoons chopped fresh basil leaves

2 teaspoons chopped fresh rosemary leaves or ⅔ teaspoon dried rosemary

2 to 3 garlic cloves, thinly sliced

2 tablespoons grated Parmesan cheese

12 large shrimp (about ¾ pound), peeled and deveined

¼ to ½ teaspoon crushed red pepper flakes

¼ cup dry white wine

Juice of 1 lemon

Place the eggs and cornmeal in two separate shallow bowls. Sprinkle the tomatoes with the salt and pepper and dip them in the eggs and then in the cornmeal.

Place a large skillet over medium-high heat and when it is hot, add the oil. Add the tomatoes and cook until they are deeply browned, about 4 to 5 minutes on each side.

Scatter the onion, basil, rosemary, garlic, Parmesan cheese, shrimp, and red pepper flakes over the tomatoes and pour the white wine over the top. Cover and cook until the shrimp is pink and opaque throughout, about 5 minutes.

Sprinkle with the lemon juice and serve immediately.

GORGONZOLA-STUFFED FIGS WITH BALSAMIC GLAZE

When we serve this dish at Olives, we roast the stuffed figs in our brick oven. The sweet skin of the fig gets charred, the meat becomes plump, the Gorgonzola oozes, and the salty-smoky flavor of the ham binds it all together. I recommend that for this dish you use only fresh Black Mission figs, which are available during the summer.

This dish can be assembled ahead of time and cooked just before serving.

SERVES 4

8 fresh Black Mission figs, quartered through the stem end, leaving the root end intact
½ cup crumbled Gorgonzola cheese (see Note)
8 paper-thin slices smoked ham
1 tablespoon olive oil
2 teaspoons finely chopped fresh rosemary leaves
½ teaspoon kosher salt
½ teaspoon black pepper
1 cup balsamic vinegar

Preheat the oven to 450 degrees.

Place the figs in a medium-size baking pan and stuff each one with 1 tablespoon Gorgonzola. Wrap each with a slice of ham and sprinkle with the oil, rosemary, salt, and pepper. Bake until the figs are gooey on the inside and charred on the outside, soft but still firm, about 15 to 18 minutes.

Meanwhile, place the vinegar in a small saucepan and bring to a boil over high heat. Continue boiling until it reduces to about ¼ cup, about 10 minutes. As soon as the figs come out of the oven, pour the hot glaze over them. Serve immediately.

NOTE: *You can substitute Roquefort, Danish blue, or ricotta cheese for the Gorgonzola.*

CRAZY MUSHROOM SALAD

Chris Moran, my former sous chef, dubbed this salad "crazy" because we try to include as many different types of mushrooms as we can and because when it's on the menu, we sell a huge amount, which makes for a very hectic kitchen. (We don't call it "wild" mushroom salad because unless mushrooms are found in the forest, they're cultivated.)

I'm not really a fan of raw mushrooms; in fact, the raw mushroom craze is something I've never understood. If they're sliced paper-thin and served with lots of shaved Parmesan, I can handle it. Otherwise, as far as I'm concerned, the only thing to do is cook them. I particularly love the combination of textures and flavors in this dish, achieved by using so many kinds of mushrooms.

Serve these as a starter for a Simple Roasted Chicken for Two (page 244).

SERVES 4

6 tablespoons olive oil
2 garlic cloves, thinly sliced
1 cup trimmed oyster mushrooms
8 shiitake mushrooms, trimmed and wiped clean
2 tablespoons sherry
1 sprig fresh rosemary
1 tablespoon chopped ham
1 shallot, thinly sliced
1 cup water
4 fresh morels, trimmed and wiped clean
1 teaspoon coarsely grated lemon zest
2 bay leaves
1 tablespoon balsamic vinegar
1 tablespoon sherry vinegar

Juice of 1 lemon
2 tablespoons chopped scallion greens
¾ teaspoon Dijon mustard

Place a large skillet over medium-high heat and when it is hot, add 1 tablespoon of the olive oil. Add the garlic and oyster and shiitake mushrooms, stirring well after each addition, and cook until softened, about 2 minutes. Add the sherry, rosemary, ham, shallot, and water, stirring well after each addition, and simmer for 2 minutes. Add the morels and cook for 10 minutes. Add the lemon zest and bay leaves and cook until the liquid has evaporated, about 15 minutes.

Stir in the remaining 5 tablespoons oil and cook for 10 minutes. Add the balsamic vinegar, sherry vinegar, lemon juice, scallions, and mustard. Let cool and remove the rosemary sprig.

Scatter the mushrooms across the plates or arrange each variety in its own pile. Serve at room temperature.

FOIE GRAS AND BLACK TRUFFLE FLAN WITH WILD MUSHROOM RAGÙ AND MÂCHE

*T*his is an ultimate indulgence, to be enjoyed when your budget, either caloric or cash, is not a consideration. Unbelievably rich and intense, yet somehow also light and smooth, this flan is a perfect starter to any steak dish.

SERVES 4

2 cups heavy cream

4 ounces raw foie gras, finely chopped (available at specialty food shops or by mail order, see page 351)

1 ounce fresh, canned, or frozen black truffle

5 large egg yolks

1 teaspoon kosher salt

½ teaspoon black pepper

1 teaspoon truffle oil (optional)

WILD MUSHROOM RAGÙ:

1 tablespoon unsalted butter

⅔ to ¾ pound assorted mushrooms, such as shiitake, portobello, hedgehog, and/or yellow-foot chanterelles, trimmed and wiped clean

1 shallot, diced

1 tablespoon red wine or ruby port

1 cup Chicken Broth (page 38), Dark Stock (page 40), or canned low-sodium chicken broth

1 teaspoon fresh thyme leaves

½ teaspoon kosher salt

¼ teaspoon black pepper

4 bunches mâche (lamb's lettuce) or 4 sprigs chervil

Preheat the oven to 325 degrees. Butter four ¾-cup flan or soufflé molds.

Place ½ cup of the cream and the foie gras in a blender or food processor and process just until blended. Pass the mixture through a fine strainer into a stainless steel bowl. Discard the solids.

Place ½ cup of the cream and the truffles in the food processor or blender and process briefly. Transfer to the bowl with the foie gras. Add the remaining 1 cup cream, the egg yolks, salt, pepper, and, if desired, the truffle oil and blend until well incorporated. Pour into the prepared molds and place in a larger pan filled with enough water to come halfway up the sides of the molds. Bake until the flans are firm to the touch, about 45 minutes.

To make the ragù: Melt the butter in a large skillet over medium heat. Add the mushrooms and shallot and cook until the mushrooms are golden and tender, about 10 minutes. Add the wine and scrape the browned bits from the bottom of the pan. Add the stock, thyme, salt, and pepper and simmer until reduced to a saucelike consistency, about 10 minutes.

To serve, divide the ragù among four plates, spreading the mushrooms out evenly. Carefully unmold the flan on top of the ragù by running a knife around the sides. Garnish each plate with the mâche or chervil. Serve warm.

Parmesan Pudding with Sweet Pea Sauce

*S*everal years ago, Olivia and I were in Italy. When we saw this dish on the menu, we were intrigued, and after we ate it, we were completely delighted. When I got back to the States, I tried to recreate the amazing flavor combination. It has become a springtime staple at Olives, arriving on the menu as soon as fresh peas are in season.

SERVES 6 TO 8

1 tablespoon unsalted butter
2 tablespoons all-purpose flour
¾ cup light cream
¼ cup whole milk
¾ cup heavy cream
1 large egg
2 large egg yolks
⅔ cup finely grated Parmesan cheese
¼ teaspoon kosher salt
⅛ teaspoon black pepper

PEA SAUCE:
1½ cups fresh or defrosted frozen sweet peas
¾ cup Chicken Broth (page 38) or canned low-sodium chicken broth
3 tablespoons heavy cream
¼ teaspoon kosher salt
⅛ teaspoon black pepper
Pea shoots, for garnish (optional)

Preheat the oven to 250 degrees. Butter a miniature (3-x-6) bread pan and line it with parchment paper.

Melt the butter in a medium-size saucepan and whisk in the flour. Continue whisking until the mixture is bubbling and has the consistency of mashed potatoes. Slowly whisk in the light cream.

Off the heat, slowly add the milk, heavy cream, egg, and egg yolks, whisking well after each addition. Add the Parmesan cheese, stirring until fully incorporated. Stir in the salt and pepper.

Pour the pudding into the prepared pan and place the pan in a larger pan filled with enough water to come halfway up the sides of the bread pan. Cover with aluminum foil, gently place in the oven, and bake for about 2 hours. When the pudding is done, it will be somewhat firm and a knife inserted in the center will come out clean. Let cool, then cover and refrigerate overnight.

To make the pea sauce: Place the peas, chicken broth, cream, salt, and pepper in a blender and blend until smooth. Set aside. The pea sauce can be made ahead, covered, and refrigerated.

Place the sauce in a small saucepan over very low heat and cook until warm, about 1 to 2 minutes.

To serve, unmold the pudding onto a cutting board. Cut into 6 to 8 slices and place each slice in the center of a heatproof plate. Place the plates in the oven and heat until the pudding is just warm, about 2 to 3 minutes.

Pour the sauce around the pudding slices and garnish with the pea tendrils, if desired.

LENTIL HUMMUS

Hummus is a Mediterranean dish traditionally made with chick peas (garbanzo beans) and sesame tahini. Everyone makes it a little differently; one version is abundant with tahini while another is abundant with olive oil and garlic. Instead of playing with the amounts of the ingredients, I started experimenting with the ingredients themselves, in particular, different legumes. I'm certainly not the first to reinterpret this classic, but I think this hummus made with lentils is among the best I've had.

Serve this as a dip with pita toasts or crudités or as a spread for a grilled swordfish or salmon sandwich.

- *Wash lentils in a colander or a strainer under cold running water. Be sure to get rid of any pebbles and dust—keep rinsing the lentils until the water runs clear.*

MAKES ABOUT 1 CUP

¼ cup olive oil, plus more for garnish
1 small carrot, peeled and diced
½ Spanish onion, diced
3 garlic cloves, chopped
1 small celery stalk, diced
¼ to ½ teaspoon crushed red pepper flakes
½ cinnamon stick
5 tablespoons chopped fresh cilantro leaves
1 cup brown lentils, rinsed and picked over
1½ tablespoons chopped fresh rosemary leaves or ½ tablespoon
   dried rosemary
4 cups water

1 to 1½ teaspoons honey, depending on how sweet you like it
1 tablespoon sesame tahini
2 teaspoons kosher salt
1 teaspoon black pepper
¼ cup chopped scallions, for garnish

Place a medium-size saucepan over medium-high heat and when it is hot, add 2 tablespoons of the oil. Add the carrot, onion, garlic, celery, pepper flakes, cinnamon stick, and 2 tablespoons of the cilantro, stirring well after each addition. Cook until the onion is soft, about 5 minutes, stirring occasionally.

Add the lentils, rosemary, and water and bring to a boil. Reduce the heat to low and cook until the lentils are very soft and the mixture is thick, about 1½ hours.

Remove the cinnamon stick and add the remaining 2 tablespoons of olive oil and the honey, tahini, salt, and black pepper. Transfer the mixture to a food processor fitted with a steel blade and puree until completely smooth. Place the mixture in a fine-wire-mesh strainer and strain into a bowl, pressing with the back of a wooden spoon. Discard the solids.

Place in a serving bowl and drizzle olive oil over the top. Garnish with the remaining 3 tablespoons cilantro and the chopped scallions.

White Bean and Roasted Garlic Hummus with Warm Rosemary Oil

*W*hite Bean and Roasted Garlic Hummus is a great dip for grilled shrimp, cut-up vegetables, and toasted bread triangles. It's also delicious on a sandwich of fresh beefsteak tomatoes, Cheddar cheese, and avocado slices.

MAKES ABOUT 1½ CUPS

¼ cup olive oil
1 medium-size Spanish onion, thinly sliced
3 garlic cloves, pressed or thinly sliced
½ teaspoon ground cumin
2½ cups cooked white cannellini beans, rinsed
2 bay leaves
1 cup water
3 tablespoons fresh lemon juice, or additional to taste (about ¾ lemon)
1 bulb roasted garlic (see page 28), peeled
⅓ cup sesame tahini
2 to 3 teaspoons kosher salt
2 teaspoons chopped fresh rosemary leaves
Shaved or grated Parmesan cheese, for garnish

Place a medium-size saucepan over medium-high heat and when it is hot, add 1 tablespoon of the oil. Add the onion, garlic, and cumin and cook until the onion is soft, about 5 minutes. Add the beans, bay leaves, and water. Bring to a boil and cook for about 5 minutes. Reduce the heat to low and cook until the beans are very soft and the mixture is thick, about 20 minutes.

Remove the bay leaves and add 1 tablespoon olive oil, the lemon juice, roasted garlic, and tahini. Transfer the mixture to a food processor fitted with a steel blade and puree until completely smooth.

Place the mixture in a fine-wire-mesh strainer and strain into a bowl, pressing with the back of a wooden spoon. Discard the solids.

Add the salt and, if desired, additional lemon juice to taste.

To make the rosemary oil: Place the remaining 2 tablespoons olive oil and the rosemary in a small skillet over low heat and cook until just warm, about 5 minutes.

Place the hummus in a small serving bowl and serve drizzled with the rosemary oil and sprinkled with Parmesan cheese.

ARTICHOKE GUACAMOLE

$\mathcal{T}$his recipe happened by accident when one of the cooks at Olives over-cooked a batch of artichoke bottoms. The texture reminded me of ripe avo-cado, so I thought it would be a fun play on guacamole and, at the same time, cut the fat and calories.

Artichoke Guacamole is best served as a condiment, scooped onto cros-tini or grilled chicken, steak, or salmon.

MAKES ABOUT 1½ CUPS

6 large fresh, frozen, or canned artichoke bottoms, including stem except
for ½ inch (see instructions on page 67 for fresh artichokes)
½ small red onion, finely chopped
1 large beefsteak tomato, chopped
2 tablespoons fresh lemon juice (about ½ lemon)
3 tablespoons extra-virgin olive oil
1 teaspoon toasted sesame oil
⅓ cup chopped scallions
3 tablespoons chopped fresh cilantro leaves
1 teaspoon kosher salt
½ teaspoon black pepper

Place the artichoke bottoms in a small saucepan, cover with water, and bring to a boil over high heat. Reduce the heat to medium-low and cook until the artichokes are very soft, about 20 minutes. Drain.

When they are cool enough to handle, finely chop the artichokes and place in a medium-size mixing bowl. Add the onion, tomato, lemon juice, olive oil, sesame oil, scallions, cilantro, salt, and pepper and gently mash with a fork.

Soups ∎

CHESTNUT SOUP
WITH A HONEY LECHE DULCE

*T*his unusual, slightly sweet, very rich soup should be served in small portions.

MAKES ABOUT 6 CUPS, SERVING 6

LECHE DULCE:
¼ cup honey
2 cups apple cider
1 Spanish onion, thinly sliced
1 cup heavy cream

4 cups Chicken Broth (page 38) or canned low-sodium chicken broth
2 cups peeled fresh, canned, or frozen chestnuts (see page 204)
1 teaspoon kosher salt
½ teaspoon black pepper

To make the leche dulce: Place the honey and apple cider in a medium-size saucepan and bring to a boil over medium-high heat. Cook for 5 minutes. Add the onion and cook for 3 minutes. Add the cream and cook until the onions are caramelized and the liquid is reduced by half, about 20 minutes.

Add the broth and chestnuts and bring to a boil. Add the salt and pepper. Transfer the mixture to a blender and process until smooth.

Serve in small portions in shallow bowls.

PAPA AL POMODORO WITH PAN-ROASTED SHRIMP AND WHITE BEANS

*T*his is a classic example of what I love about Italian regional cooking. Papa al Pomodoro was probably first prepared in desperation as a way to stretch the family's daily food, an incredibly creative, resourceful, and delicious solution.

The freshness of the ingredients is critical to the success of this dish. Although it's okay to use canned tomatoes, this soup is best in the summer or early fall, when fresh tomatoes are at their ripest. The flavor of the dish is completely dependent on the quality of the tomatoes and the silky texture on the quality of the bread, so be sure to use a country-style bread or peasant loaf.

You can omit the Pan-Roasted Shrimp and White Beans, but the soup is a great vehicle for the sweet, meaty flavor of the shrimp.

SERVES 8 AS AN APPETIZER, 4 AS AN ENTRÉE

1 Spanish onion, chopped
1 anchovy fillet, chopped
16 plum tomatoes, fresh or canned, drained if canned
2 tablespoons olive oil
4 garlic cloves, roughly chopped
2 tablespoons chopped fresh rosemary leaves or ⅔ teaspoon dried rosemary
3 cups Chicken Broth (page 38) or canned low-sodium chicken broth
4 cups cubes dense rustic bread (trimmed of crust and cut into 2-inch cubes)

PAN-ROASTED SHRIMP AND WHITE BEANS:
20 large shrimp, peeled and deveined
1 teaspoon kosher salt
½ teaspoon black pepper

1 tablespoon olive oil
1 garlic clove, minced
1 cup cooked white cannellini beans, rinsed
½ cup chopped fresh flat-leaf parsley leaves
¼ cup chopped fresh basil leaves

Shaved or grated Parmesan cheese, for garnish

Preheat the oven to 450 degrees.

Place a large ovenproof skillet over medium-high heat and when it is hot, add the onion, anchovy, and tomatoes. Cook, turning the tomatoes and stirring the onions and anchovies, until the tomato skins are browned and wrinkled—about 5 minutes, 3 to 4 minutes if using canned tomatoes.

Stir in the oil, garlic, and rosemary and transfer to the oven. Bake for 15 minutes.

Return the skillet to medium heat, add the chicken broth and bread cubes, and simmer until the liquid has been absorbed by the bread and the soup has a silky texture, about 10 minutes.

Place the soup in a food processor fitted with a steel blade and pulse until the ingredients are coarsely chopped but not pureed. Place in a bowl, cover, and refrigerate until thoroughly chilled, at least 1 hour. If you prefer to serve the soup hot, reheat gently before you start cooking the shrimp.

To make the shrimp and white beans: Sprinkle the shrimp with the salt and pepper. Place a large skillet over medium-high heat and when it is hot, add the oil. Add the garlic and cook until it is lightly toasted, about 2 to 3 minutes. Add the shrimp, beans, parsley, and basil, stirring well after each addition, and cook until the shrimp is pink and opaque throughout, about 3 minutes.

Ladle the soup into shallow bowls. Spoon the hot shrimp mixture over the hot or chilled soup and garnish with Parmesan cheese.

NOTE: *The texture of the soup will be somewhat thicker if served cold rather than hot; if desired, you can add additional stock to thin it slightly.*

PAPA CARCIOFI

*O*ne day we were making artichoke soup at Olives. I poured it over bread, and Papa Carciofi, inspired by Papa al Pomodoro (page 96), was born.

SERVES 4 TO 6 AS AN APPETIZER

1 tablespoon extra-virgin olive oil, plus additional for garnish (optional)
1 tablespoon chopped garlic
½ Spanish onion, thinly sliced
1 heaping tablespoon chopped prosciutto (optional)
6 large fresh artichoke bottoms (see page 67 for instructions), chopped
2½ cups Chicken Broth (page 38) or canned low-sodium chicken broth
1½ cups cubes day-old bread (use a hearty peasant loaf) (½-inch cubes)
2 tablespoons chopped fresh basil leaves
¼ cup finely grated Parmesan cheese, plus additional for garnish

Place a large cast-iron skillet over medium heat and when it is hot, add the oil. Add the garlic, the onion, and the prosciutto, if desired, stirring well after each addition, and cook until the onion has softened but has not colored, about 2 to 3 minutes. Add the artichokes and cook for 2 minutes. Add the chicken broth, increase the heat to medium-high, bring to a low boil, and cook until the artichokes are soft, 5 to 7 minutes. Add the bread cubes. Cook for 2 minutes.

Add the basil and Parmesan cheese, transfer to a blender or a food processor fitted with a steel blade, and process until smooth.

Serve hot or chilled, in small bowls, sprinkled with Parmesan and, if desired, drizzled with extra-virgin olive oil.

SWEET POTATO SOUP

*S*ometimes, all of a sudden, I just have to have a sweet potato. And when I do, I always ask myself why I don't eat them more often. This soup is a showcase for the sweet potato. Perfect for the fall, it's sweet, spicy, and creamy. Serve it as a starter to simply grilled pork chops.

MAKES 8 TO 10 CUPS

3 sweet potatoes or yams, scrubbed and pierced several times with the tines of a fork
1 tablespoon plus 2 teaspoons olive oil
1½ teaspoons kosher salt
1 teaspoon black pepper
1 Spanish onion, chopped
3 fresh sage leaves, chopped, or ½ teaspoon dried sage
1 tablespoon minced peeled fresh ginger
4 cups water
2½ cups apple cider
2 cinnamon sticks
½ teaspoon toasted sesame oil
2 fresh figs, quartered
2 tablespoons unsweetened Thai coconut milk (see Note)

YOGURT AND FIG GARNISH:
¼ cup honey
4 fresh figs, halved and thinly sliced
⅔ cup plain yogurt
4 scallions, thinly sliced
2 teaspoons chopped fresh cilantro leaves
2 teaspoons chopped fresh mint leaves

Preheat the oven to 425 degrees.

Rub the sweet potatoes with 2 teaspoons of the olive oil, ½ teaspoon of the salt, and ½ teaspoon of the pepper. Place them directly on a rack in the oven and roast until they are tender, about 40 minutes. When they are cool enough to handle, halve, scoop out the flesh, and discard the skin. Set aside.

Place a stockpot over medium-high heat and when it is hot, add the remaining 1 tablespoon olive oil. Add the onion, sage, ginger, and sweet potatoes, stirring well after each addition. Cook for 2 minutes. Add the water, apple cider, cinnamon sticks, sesame oil, figs, and the remaining 1 teaspoon salt and ½ teaspoon pepper. Cook for 20 minutes, or until the potatoes are tender.

Discard the cinnamon sticks and transfer the soup to a blender. Add the coconut milk and puree until smooth.

Meanwhile, to make the garnish: Place a skillet over medium-high heat. Add the honey and figs and cook until the figs caramelize, about 2 to 3 minutes. Remove from heat. Add the yogurt, scallions, cilantro, and mint, and mix well. Remove from the heat.

Ladle the soup into bowls and spoon a dollop of the garnish onto each one. (The soup can be refrigerated for up to 3 days.)

NOTE: *Thai coconut milk is available at well-stocked grocery stores and gourmet or Asian markets.*

ROASTED ONION SOUP

*T*his is a variation of the classic French onion soup. I've omitted the cheese gratin and toasted bread on top, but if you want more substance to this dish, pour the soup over slices of toasted bread—covered with Gruyère.

MAKES 10 TO 12 CUPS

2 tablespoons olive oil
½ cup chopped slab bacon or chopped high-quality thick-sliced lean bacon
16 garlic cloves, thinly sliced
1 chicken, about 2½ pounds, cut into serving pieces
1 ham hock or ham bone
5 white onions, thinly sliced
8 large red onions, peeled and thinly sliced
4 leeks, well washed and thinly sliced
4 tablespoons fresh rosemary leaves or 4 teaspoons dried rosemary
3 bay leaves
10 cups Chicken Broth (page 38) or canned low-sodium chicken broth

Place a large stockpot over medium-high heat and when it is hot, add the oil. Add the bacon and cook until it begins to render its fat, about 3 minutes. Add the garlic and cook until it is lightly toasted, about 2 to 3 minutes. Add the chicken, skin side down, and the ham bone and stir well. Cook until the chicken is just brown on both sides, about 5 minutes.

Add the white onions, red onions, and leeks in several batches, stirring well after each addition. Reduce the heat to medium-low, add 3 tablespoons fresh or 3 teaspoons dried rosemary and the 3 bay leaves, and cook until the onions are well browned and soft, about 20 to 25 minutes.

Increase the heat to medium, add the chicken broth, and simmer for 30 minutes.

Discard the chicken pieces and the ham bone (the chicken will be too overcooked to use in another dish). Add the remaining tablespoon chopped rosemary or the remaining teaspoon dried and cook until the liquid has reduced by one third, about 20 minutes. Serve immediately. (The soup can be refrigerated for up to 3 days.)

COCONUT AND CRAB BISQUE

I don't usually use coconut and lemon grass, but hey, they taste great. My rule for adapting a classic is, If it doesn't stray too far from the original concept, and it tastes good, it's okay by me.

MAKES 6 TO 8 SERVINGS

BROTH:
2 tablespoons olive oil
*4 crabs, in the shell, cleaned and chopped (use a cleaver or have the
    fishmonger do it for you)*
8 stalks lemon grass, cut in half lengthwise and thinly sliced (see Note)
2 tablespoons chopped peeled fresh ginger
1 cup unsweetened coconut flakes (available at health food stores)
3 celery stalks, chopped
1 red onion, sliced
1 Thai chile or jalapeño pepper, chopped
2 teaspoons ground coriander
2 teaspoons curry powder
4 cups Chicken Broth (page 38) or canned low-sodium chicken broth
4 cups water
*1¼ cups canned unsweetened Thai coconut milk (available at specialty
    food stores and Asian markets)*

GARNISH:
2 tablespoons olive oil
½ fennel bulb, trimmed, cored, quartered, and thinly sliced
2 tablespoons finely grated peeled fresh ginger
Greens from ½ bunch scallions, thinly sliced on the bias

½ cup light or heavy cream
3 tablespoons chopped fresh basil leaves
3 tablespoons chopped fresh cilantro leaves
½ to 1 pound cooked crabmeat, picked over

To make the broth: Place a 14-inch skillet over medium-high heat and when it is hot, add the oil. Add the crabs and cook for 3 minutes. Add the lemon grass, ginger, coconut, celery, onion, chile, coriander, curry, chicken broth, water, and coconut milk, stirring well after each addition, and bring to a low boil. Reduce the heat to low and simmer for 35 minutes. Strain the broth and discard the solids. (The broth can be made ahead and refrigerated for up to 24 hours or frozen for 2 months.)

To make the garnish: Place a medium-size stockpot over medium heat and when it is hot, add the oil. Add the fennel, ginger, and scallions and cook until the ginger is golden and the fennel is soft, about 3 minutes.

Add the crab broth and cream and cook until heated through, about 2 minutes. Add the basil, cilantro, and crabmeat. Bring to a simmer and cook until the crab is heated through, about 3 minutes. Serve immediately.

NOTE: *If you cannot find lemon grass, add an additional 2 tablespoons chopped peeled ginger.*

LITTLENECK CLAM
AND SWEET CARROT BISQUE

*T*his bisque started out as a dish of carrot-flavored spaghetti with littleneck clams and bacon, and later evolved into a sauce for swordfish. Further simplified, it becomes this bisque. If you want even more simplicity, omit the clams.

Unless you're allergic to sesame, don't omit the sesame oil: the tiny amount really makes a difference in the flavor of the soup.

SERVES 8 AS AN APPETIZER OR 4 AS AN ENTRÉE

4 carrots, peeled and quartered
4 cups water, Chicken Broth (page 38), or canned low-sodium
  chicken broth
4 thick slices high-quality lean bacon, chopped
1 Spanish onion, chopped
2 tablespoons finely minced peeled fresh ginger
3 to 4 garlic cloves, chopped
32 littleneck clams, scrubbed
¾ cup orange juice
½ cup dry white wine
1 tablespoon Pernod or Ricard (optional)
½ teaspoon toasted sesame oil
1 teaspoon kosher salt
½ teaspoon black pepper
¼ cup light or heavy cream (optional)
1 bunch scallions, chopped, for garnish
¼ cup chopped fresh cilantro leaves, for garnish

Place the carrots and water in a medium saucepan and bring to a boil over high heat. Reduce the heat to medium and cook at a low boil until the carrots are very soft, about 20 minutes. Transfer the mixture to a blender and puree. Set aside.

Place a large skillet over medium-high heat and add the bacon, onion, ginger, garlic, and clams, stirring well after each addition. Cook for 3 minutes, or until the bacon has rendered its fat. Add the reserved carrot puree, orange juice, wine, and, if desired, the Pernod. Continue cooking until the clams open, about 12 minutes. Discard any clams that do not open.

Take the pan off the heat and add the sesame oil, salt, pepper, and, if desired, the cream. Reheat gently, if necessary. Garnish with the scallions and cilantro.

ASPARAGUS SOUP WITH OREGANO AND FETA CHEESE

When I was very young, asparagus was like artichokes and caviar, a special-occasion food. When I was a teenager, my family moved into a house that had a substantial vegetable garden, and I planted potatoes, several kinds of tomatoes, and greens. The first spring, I discovered some funny-looking green spears shooting up through the earth. At first I didn't know what they were, but when I realized that they were asparagus, I harvested and cooked them— and wow! They were like no asparagus I'd ever tasted. Now asparagus is as common as green beans, but I try to use it only when it's in season.

If asparagus is out of season, you can substitute broccoli for the asparagus.

■ *When buying asparagus, look for thin, firm, bright green stalks; avoid any that are dry-looking. Be sure that all the asparagus are about the same thickness to ensure even cooking.*

MAKES ABOUT 10 CUPS

2 pounds asparagus, peeled, woody portion of the stem trimmed off and discarded
3 tablespoons olive oil, plus ¼ cup additional (optional)
1 large Spanish onion, thinly sliced
4 garlic cloves, thinly sliced
1 Idaho potato, peeled and diced
8 cups water, Chicken Broth (page 38), or canned low-sodium chicken broth
1 tablespoon chopped fresh oregano leaves or 1 teaspoon dried oregano, preferably Greek
1 cup crumbled feta cheese

Bring a large pot of water to a boil. Add the asparagus and cook until it turns bright green, about 3 minutes. Drain and plunge into a bowl of ice water. Drain again. Cut off the tips and set the tips and the stalks aside separately.

Place a large skillet over medium-low heat and when it is hot, add 2 tablespoons of the olive oil. Add the onion and garlic and cook until soft and almost translucent, about 20 minutes. Add the potato, water or chicken broth, and oregano, increase the heat to high, and bring to a boil. Reduce the heat to medium and cook until the potato is tender, about 20 minutes.

Add the asparagus stalks and transfer the mixture to a blender. Blend until completely smooth, gradually adding the ¼ cup olive oil, if desired, to enrich the soup.

Place a medium-size skillet over medium-high heat and when it is hot, add the remaining 1 tablespoon olive oil. Add the reserved asparagus tips and cook for 1 minute. Add the feta cheese and cook for 1 minute, allowing it to melt slightly.

Ladle the soup into bowls and garnish with the asparagus-feta mixture.

CARL'S PAGODA–INSPIRED TOMATO SOUP

$\mathcal{M}$y inspiration for this dish was a soup I had at a restaurant in Boston's China-town called Carl's Pagoda. Tomato soup is definitely not something you think of as Chinese or even Asian; Carl's soup was served warm with lots of sautéed tomatoes and it just wowed me. I only make this soup with ripe tomatoes in the late summer and early fall.

This soup can be served hot with grilled shrimp or steamed clams, or chilled with Tuna Tartare (page 62).

MAKES ABOUT 8 CUPS

1 tablespoon olive oil
2 Spanish onions, roughly chopped
8 to 10 medium beefsteak tomatoes, roughly chopped
3 tablespoons chopped peeled fresh ginger
4 garlic cloves, chopped
⅓ cup soy sauce
1 tablespoon fish sauce
2 tablespoons toasted sesame oil
½ to 1 teaspoon chopped Scotch bonnet, jalapeño,
 or Thai chile pepper
¼ cup white sugar
¼ cup chopped scallion greens, for garnish
¼ cup chopped fresh cilantro leaves, for garnish

Place a large skillet over medium-high flame and when it is hot, add the oil. Add the onions, tomatoes, ginger, and garlic, stirring well after each addition, and cook until the onions and garlic are lightly browned, about 7 minutes. Add the soy sauce, fish sauce, sesame oil, chile, and sugar, stirring well after each addition, and cook until slightly reduced, about 15 minutes.

Transfer the soup to a food processor fitted with a steel blade and process until smooth. Strain and discard the seeds and pulp. Reheat if necessary.

Garnish each serving with scallions and cilantro.

SALADS ∎

BIBB LETTUCE WITH A SHOWER OF ROQUEFORT CHEESE

*M*y favorite lettuces are either tender, bitter, or crunchy. I don't like to mix them. This is my tender lettuce salad—my preference is to use only Bibb, but if you prefer you can add other tender leaves, like mâche or Boston lettuce. The hot dressing will wilt the lettuce slightly: it's supposed to.

■ *T I P*

To achieve a "shower" of Roquefort cheese, first place the cheese in the freezer for at least 20 minutes. Put a chunk in a rotary cheese grater and grate onto the lettuce.

SERVES 4

2 tablespoons walnut oil
⅔ cup chopped walnuts
2 tablespoons fresh lemon juice (about ½ lemon)
Splash of balsamic vinegar
2 heads Bibb lettuce, well washed, dried, and torn into bite-size pieces
¼ white onion, very thinly sliced
1 teaspoon kosher salt
½ teaspoon black pepper
½ cup shaved or crumbled Roquefort cheese (about 2½ ounces)

Place a small skillet over medium-high heat and when it is hot, add the oil. Add the walnuts and cook until they are lightly toasted, about 3 minutes. Off the heat, add the lemon juice and vinegar.

In a large bowl, mix the lettuce, onion, salt, and pepper.

Divide the lettuce among 4 plates and pour the hot dressing over it. Add the Roquefort cheese and serve immediately.

FRESH TUNA TABOULI

When I traveled to Israel and the Mideast, I always loved watching the techniques and flavors used for making the different salads. When I saw lamb being used for tabouli, I immediately thought of tuna and what a fun idea it would be to use it that way.

Although you can find tabouli in almost every Middle Eastern country, the origins are thought to be Lebanese. Traditional tabouli is made with cracked wheat, parsley, fresh mint, scallions, tomatoes, olive oil, and lemon juice.

SERVES 4

⅓ cup coarse bulgur wheat
½ cup boiling water
1 large cucumber, peeled, seeded, and minced
1 tablespoon finely chopped peeled fresh ginger
1 shallot, minced
1 heaping tablespoon chopped fresh mint leaves
1 heaping tablespoon chopped fresh cilantro leaves
½ teaspoon ground cumin
1 teaspoon kosher salt
½ teaspoon black pepper
2 to 4 tablespoons extra-virgin olive oil
1½ cups (about ¾ pound) finely chopped very fresh bluefin or yellowfin
   tuna (this must be done by hand)
2 tablespoons fresh lemon juice (about ½ lemon)
1 to 2 beefsteak tomatoes, cut into 4 thick slices

Place the bulgur and water in a large bowl and let sit for 20 minutes, then stir and cool to room temperature. The bulgur should be soft but not mushy; it should still have some bite.

Add the cucumber, ginger, shallot, mint, cilantro, cumin, salt, pepper, oil, and tuna and stir well.

Just prior to serving, add the lemon juice. Place 1 tomato slice on each plate. Using a 1-cup "dry" measuring cup, scoop up the tabouli and place 1 cup on each of the tomato slices. Serve immediately.

MARINATED ROASTED RED PEPPERS

When I was growing up, the only time I ate roasted peppers was on Thanksgiving and Christmas antipasto trays. Now my favorite way to enjoy their sweet, meaty flavor is on crostini. Serve these with Black Olive Toasts (page 61).

SERVES 5 TO 6 AS AN ACCOMPANIMENT

⅔ pound roasted red bell peppers (see page 48) (weight after roasting)
5 garlic cloves, coarsely chopped
½ bunch fresh basil leaves, roughly chopped
1½ teaspoons fresh rosemary leaves
¼ cup extra-virgin olive oil

Combine the red peppers, garlic, basil, rosemary, and olive oil in a medium-size bowl, cover, and refrigerate overnight. Serve at room temperature.

CRAB AND CUCUMBER SLAW

I originally served this dish as part of a deluxe crab tasting plate, which included Crab Ravioli, Olives Crab Cakes (page 54), Soft-Shell Crabs, and Crab-Stuffed Zucchini Blossoms, using all the different crabs from across the country: Maryland, King, Blue, and Jonah.

Use the freshest and sweetest crabs you can find. If good-quality crab is unavailable, use shrimp instead.

SERVES 4

*6 cucumbers, peeled and very thinly sliced lengthwise (use a Japanese
    mandoline if available)*
2 avocados, peeled, pitted, and cut into thick julienne
Greens from 1 bunch scallions, finely chopped
*1 carrot, peeled and very thinly sliced lengthwise (with a Japanese
    mandoline)*
2 teaspoons chopped fresh cilantro leaves
2 teaspoons chopped fresh basil leaves
Juice of 1 lemon
1 pound cooked crabmeat, picked over but not shredded
1 teaspoon kosher salt
½ teaspoon black pepper
1 tablespoon extra-virgin olive oil

Layer the cucumbers in the bottom of a large serving bowl. Layer the avocados, scallions, and carrots on top. Scatter, in the following order, the cilantro, basil, lemon juice, crabmeat, salt, pepper, and oil over the top. Serve immediately.

Roasted Red Pepper Salad

*T*his is the only salad I make with red peppers, roasted or raw. It was originally paired with Marinated Leg of Lamb Sandwich (page 277), a signature dish that was on the menu at Olives years ago. Now I serve it as an accompaniment to many dishes or as part of a mezze plate.

SERVES 4 TO 8

6 large roasted red bell peppers (see page 48), julienned
1 large red onion, thinly sliced
3 scallions, finely chopped

DRESSING:
1 garlic clove, chopped
2 tablespoons grated lemon zest
1 teaspoon Hungarian paprika
1 teaspoon ground cumin
2 teaspoons chopped fresh rosemary leaves or ⅔ teaspoon dried rosemary
¼ teaspoon turmeric
Pinch of cayenne pepper
Pinch of ground cinnamon
Pinch of ground nutmeg
1 teaspoon kosher salt
½ teaspoon black pepper
3 tablespoons fresh lemon juice
½ cup extra-virgin olive oil

Place the peppers, onion, and scallions in a medium-size salad bowl.
To make the dressing: Place all the dressing ingredients except the olive

oil in a blender or a food processor fitted with a steel blade and blend well. While the machine is running, gradually add the olive oil in a thin, steady stream and process until smooth.

Pour the dressing over the vegetables and toss to combine. Serve at room temperature.

SHAVED RAW FENNEL AND RED ONION SALAD

*F*ennel is a very common vegetable in the Mediterranean. I often chew on a stalk while I'm working in the kitchen because I find the sweet anise-like flavor refreshing. It is one of the few vegetables I enjoy both raw and cooked. I find cooked fennel is best served with seafood.

This is a great fresh, crispy salad, perfect when served, Italian-style, after a meal of grilled fish or chicken.

SERVES 4

*3 fennel bulbs, trimmed, cored, and very thinly sliced or shaved (with a
    Japanese mandoline or a meat slicer)*
1 large red onion, thinly sliced or shaved (with the mandoline or slicer)
¼ cup extra-virgin olive oil
6 tablespoons fresh lemon juice (about 1½ lemons)
2 teaspoons balsamic vinegar
2 teaspoons Dijon mustard
½ teaspoon kosher salt
½ teaspoon black pepper
1 large bunch arugula, well washed, dried, and torn into bite-size pieces
Shaved Parmesan cheese, for garnish

Combine all the ingredients except the Parmesan in a large serving bowl and toss well. Serve immediately, garnished with the shaved Parmesan cheese.

GARLIC SCAMPI AND BEAN SALAD

I have continued to embellish on the shrimp-and-bean combination since I first tasted it at a small trattoria in Tuscany. I've tried shrimp-and-bean fritters, risotto, pasta, and soups, but this hot-and-cold salad remains my favorite. The sweet and tart balsamic and sherry vinegars, combined with the sweet meat of the shrimp and the soft buttery richness of the beans, take this combination to a new level.

Serve as an entrée or luncheon salad with bread, followed by raw sliced fennel. Pretty simple, and pretty terrific.

■ *To quick-cook beans, wash them well, place them in a large pot, and cover with lots of cold water. Bring to a boil over high heat, reduce the heat to low, partially cover, and gently simmer until soft, about 2 hours. Drain and rinse well.*

SERVES 4 TO 6

BEAN SALAD:
4 cups cooked pinto or cranberry beans (about 1¾ cups dry), rinsed
1 beefsteak tomato, cut into small dice
½ fennel bulb, trimmed, cored, and cut into small dice
3 tablespoons extra-virgin olive oil
2 tablespoons fresh lemon juice (about ½ lemon)
2 tablespoons balsamic vinegar
1 teaspoon sherry vinegar
1 tablespoon Dijon mustard
¼ cup chopped fresh cilantro leaves
¼ cup chopped scallions
¼ cup chopped fresh flat-leaf parsley leaves

1 teaspoon kosher salt
½ teaspoon black pepper

GARLIC SCAMPI:
1 tablespoon olive oil
1 pound large shrimp in the shell, butterflied and deveined, with tails
*   left on*
½ teaspoon kosher salt
½ teaspoon black pepper
2 garlic cloves, thinly sliced
¼ teaspoon crushed red pepper flakes
2 large bunches arugula, well washed, dried, and torn into bite-size pieces
Shaved Parmesan cheese, for garnish

To make the bean salad: Place the beans, tomato, and fennel in a large bowl. Sprinkle with the oil, lemon juice, vinegars, mustard, cilantro, scallions, parsley, salt, and pepper and toss well. Cover and refrigerate for at least 4 hours, or overnight.

To make the garlic scampi: Place a large skillet over medium-high heat and when it is hot, add the oil. Sprinkle the shrimp with the salt and pepper and add the shrimp and garlic to the skillet. Cook until the shrimp are pink and opaque throughout, about 2 to 3 minutes.

Peel the shrimp and add to the salad. Sprinkle with the pepper flakes. Toss with the arugula and Parmesan cheese and serve immediately.

FRESH TOMATO AND CORN SALAD

My mother used to make this salad when I was a child growing up in Georgia. Every August our town had a big corn and tomato celebration, and the next day she'd always combine the two into a salad.

This is essentially Mom's salad with the addition of cilantro, which we didn't use back then.

The flavor of this salad relies heavily on the sweetness of the corn, so wait until sweet corn is in season to make it.

SERVES 4

3 beefsteak tomatoes, diced
3 tablespoons chopped fresh basil leaves
1 tablespoon chopped fresh cilantro leaves
1 small red onion, halved and thinly sliced
⅓ cup chopped scallion greens
¼ cup balsamic vinegar
1 teaspoon kosher salt
½ teaspoon black pepper
2 tablespoons extra-virgin olive oil
3 garlic cloves, thinly sliced
1 to 2 anchovy fillets, minced
4 cups fresh corn kernels
1 tablespoon Dijon mustard

Place the tomatoes, basil, cilantro, onion, scallion greens, vinegar, salt, and pepper in a large salad bowl.

Place a large skillet over medium-high heat and when it is hot, add the oil. Add the garlic and anchovies and cook until they are lightly toasted, about 2 minutes. Add the corn kernels and mustard and cook for 2 minutes, stirring constantly. Add to the tomato salad, toss, and serve immediately.

Arugula Salad with Tomato and Cucumber Juice

*A*rugula, similar to the radish leaf, is one of my favorite bitter greens. At Olives, we make this salad when someone wants a salad with no fat at all. It's delicious served with Ginger Mustard Chicken (page 256).

SERVES 4

3 bunches arugula, well washed, dried, and torn into bite-size pieces

DRESSING:
1 cucumber, peeled, seeded, and pureed, or ½ cup cucumber juice
1 tablespoon rice vinegar
Juice of ½ lemon
2 beefsteak tomatoes, finely minced
1 red onion, finely minced
4 garlic cloves, finely minced
1 tablespoon chopped fresh rosemary leaves or 1 teaspoon dried rosemary
1 tablespoon chopped fresh basil leaves or 1 teaspoon dried basil
1 teaspoon chopped fresh thyme leaves
2 teaspoons Dijon mustard
1 teaspoon kosher salt
½ teaspoon black pepper

Place the arugula in a large serving bowl.

To make the dressing: Combine the cucumber juice, vinegar, lemon juice, tomatoes, onion, garlic, rosemary, basil, thyme, mustard, salt, and pepper in a small bowl. Mix well and pour over the arugula. Toss and serve immediately.

ROQUEFORT CAESAR SALAD

Caesar salad has emerged as an American classic, showing up at casual as well as high-end restaurants. It is best, though rarely, made at the table. I am particularly fond of this version, which uses a lightly toasted anchovy-and-garlic dressing to create a warm Caesar.

What is it about Caesar salads that people love so much? Although lots of people make them, few make them well. The art of making a Caesar salad is achieving a delicate balance of flavors: if you don't get it just right, you blow the whole thing. In this rendition, the Roquefort cheese adds a lushness that you won't want to overdo. (If you don't like Roquefort, simply omit it.)

■ *A Caesar salad is not a Caesar salad without the oily, salty, strong-tasting anchovy. Usually found canned in oil or packed in salt, anchovies are sometimes available smoked or dried. They are rarely eaten fresh.*

SERVES 4 TO 6

DRESSING:
5 tablespoons olive oil
2 large anchovy fillets, minced
3 garlic cloves, thinly sliced
¼ cup coarsely chopped walnuts
¼ cup fresh lemon juice (about 1 lemon)
1 tablespoon balsamic vinegar
1 teaspoon Dijon mustard
5 tablespoons buttermilk
¼ cup chopped scallions
1 teaspoon kosher salt

1 teaspoon black pepper

2 to 3 tablespoons grated Parmesan cheese

*2 large or 3 small heads romaine lettuce, pale-green inner leaves only, well
    washed, dried, and torn into bite-size pieces*

*1½ cups croutons (made from walnut, dark rye, or whole wheat bread)
    (page 32)*

½ cup grated Roquefort cheese

2 tablespoons grated Parmesan cheese

To make the dressing: Place a large skillet over medium-high heat and
when it is hot, add 2 tablespoons of the oil. Add the anchovy fillets, garlic, and
walnuts and cook until all are golden and lightly toasted, about 2 to 3 minutes.
Remove the pan from the heat and stir in the remaining 3 tablespoons olive
oil and the lemon juice, vinegar, mustard, buttermilk, scallions, salt, pepper,
and Parmesan cheese.

Place the lettuce in a large salad bowl. Pour the warm dressing over the
lettuce, add the croutons and cheeses, and toss well. Serve immediately.

TOMATO SALAD WITH FETA CHEESE AND CUMIN

*T*his recipe, a play on Greek salad, showcases the ripe tomato. Pack this into pita bread and serve it for lunch or use it to garnish a lamb dish for dinner. I like to serve this with Pan-Fried Cornmeal-and-Cumin-Rubbed Cornish Game Hens (page 250). You can add cucumbers and Kalamata olives for a more traditional salad.

■ *Feta cheese is a crumbly ewe's-milk cheese that is usually packed in brine. I always try to use the creamiest feta I can find, typically available in Middle Eastern or Greek markets.*

SERVES 4

2 tablespoons olive oil
1 tablespoon chopped garlic
2 teaspoons ground cumin
1 tablespoon ground ginger
½ cup chopped scallions
juice of 1 lemon
6 fresh cilantro sprigs
3 tablespoons water
1 teaspoon toasted sesame oil
½ cup crumbled feta cheese
1 teaspoon kosher salt
1 teaspoon black pepper
4 beefsteak tomatoes, cubed
¼ cup chopped scallions or red onions, for garnish

Place a large skillet over medium-high heat and when it is hot, add the olive oil. Add the garlic and cumin and cook until they are lightly toasted, about 3 minutes.

Transfer the mixture to a blender, add the ginger, scallions, lemon juice, cilantro, water, sesame oil, feta cheese, salt, and pepper, and blend until smooth. Place the tomatoes in a large serving bowl, add the dressing, and garnish with the scallions.

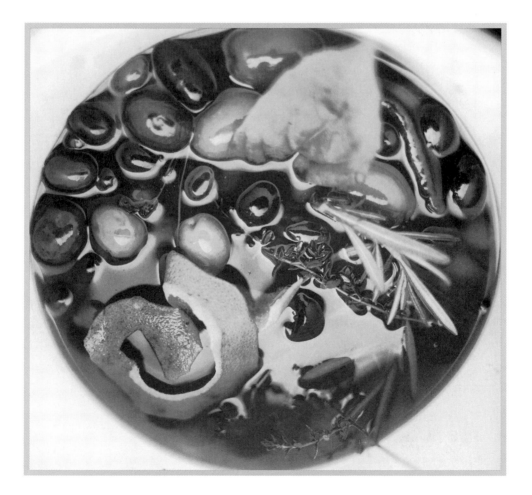

SIMPLE POACHED TUNA WITH SUMMER VINE-RIPE TOMATO SALAD

*B*ecause this salad is so simple, you must start with high-quality ingredients. The tuna *must* be cooked rare, or it will be tasteless and tough.

This is wonderful paired with the Black Olive Spaghetti Salad (page 212). Place the spaghetti salad in a large shallow bowl, make a well in the middle, and fill with the Tuna Salad.

SERVES 4

1 beefsteak or 2 plum tomatoes, diced
2 shallots, diced
2 to 3 tablespoons chopped fresh basil leaves
1 tablespoon chopped fresh cilantro leaves
1 tablespoon extra-virgin olive oil
1 to 2 tablespoons fresh lemon juice (to taste)
1½ teaspoons kosher salt
⅔ cup water
⅓ cup dry white wine
¾ to 1 pound very fresh bluefin or yellowfin tuna
¼ teaspoon black pepper

Place the tomato, shallots, basil, cilantro, olive oil, lemon juice, and 1 teaspoon of the salt in a large bowl.

Place the water and wine in a large sauté pan and bring to a boil. Sprinkle the tuna with the remaining ½ teaspoon salt and the pepper and place in the pan. Cook until the tuna is rare, about 1 minute. While the tuna is still warm, coarsely chop it and add to the tomato mixture. Toss gently, and serve immediately.

NOTE: *You can substitute the same amount of diced fresh buffalo mozzarella cheese for the poached tuna.*

VEGETABLES ▪

BASIC ROASTED VEGETABLES

*Y*ou can cook just about any vegetable this way, either alone or in combination. This recipe calls for my favorites, asparagus and broccoli. Root vegetables, such as potatoes or carrots, can be cooked in the same way with delicious results. Softer vegetables, such as tomatoes and zucchini, will need a little less time.

SERVES 4

2 bunches asparagus or broccoli, woody ends trimmed off
and discarded
1 to 2 tablespoons olive oil
1 teaspoon kosher salt
½ teaspoon black pepper
1 to 2 tablespoons fresh herbs, such as rosemary, basil, oregano, thyme,
and/or sage

Preheat the oven to 450 degrees.

Place the vegetables on a large baking sheet and sprinkle with the olive oil, salt, pepper, and herbs. Place in the oven and roast until the vegetables are well browned and tender, about 45 minutes to 1 hour.

FRESH CREAMED CORN AND BREAD PUDDING

I've always been a big fan of sweet bread puddings. Lately, I've been using the same technique to come up with something more savory, to be used as an accompaniment to an entreé. This one was inspired by a sweet corn bread pudding we made for dessert.

This makes a delicious Sunday supper paired with some roast country ham. It's also a treat for brunch or lunch, served with a simple green salad.

SERVES 6

¼ cup chopped slab bacon
¼ Spanish onion, chopped
2 cups fresh corn kernels
1 cup heavy cream
½ cup Chicken Broth (page 38), canned low-sodium chicken broth,
*   or Corn Stock (page 44)*
1 cup ½-inch cubes day-old bread
2 large eggs
½ cup milk
1½ teaspoons chopped fresh thyme leaves or ½ teaspoon dried thyme
1 teaspoon kosher salt
½ teaspoon black pepper

Preheat the oven to 300 degrees. Lightly butter an 8 x 8-inch baking pan and line with wax paper.

Place a large saucepan over medium heat and when it is hot, add the bacon. Cook until it has rendered its fat. Pour off the excess fat, if necessary, add the onion, and cook until golden, about 3 minutes. Add the corn, cream, and broth, increase the heat to medium-high, and bring to a low boil. Cook until the mixture just begins to thicken, about 7 to 10 minutes.

Transfer the corn mixture to a bowl. Add the bread, eggs, milk, thyme, salt, and pepper and stir to combine.

Scrape the mixture into the prepared pan and bake until the custard is set, about 1 hour and 15 minutes. Cut into squares or simply scoop out of the pan.

FRESH SPRING FAVA BEAN PUREE

I originally created this puree as a filling for ravioli but I liked it so much I decided to serve it on its own. The next day home alone with my then nine-month-old daughter, Isabelle, I warmed it up for her and discovered that it made great baby food.

Do not substitute lima beans or canned fava beans.

Protein-rich fava beans, also known as broad beans, have a smooth, buttery texture and a slightly bitter yet sweet, nutty flavor. I love the padded velvety pod that the beans are wrapped in and the tight little casing that protects each one. They are wrapped so well they seem like little gift packages. Nature knows that the best things in life take love and tender care to prepare; you'll find that it's really worth it to prepare the fresh beans. Fava beans have recently become more available in the United States, typically in the late spring and early summer. Look for those that are unblemished and bright green.

SERVES 6

Pinch of kosher salt
2 pounds fresh fava beans (approximately 2 cups), shucked
3 Idaho potatoes, peeled and cubed
1 small white onion, chopped
3 garlic cloves, thinly sliced
1 cup low-fat milk
1 teaspoon chopped fresh thyme leaves, plus more for garnish
Shaved Parmesan cheese, for garnish

Fill a large bowl with ice water.

Bring a pot of water to a boil over high heat and add the salt. Drop the beans into the pot, let the water return to a boil, and cook until the beans are bright green, about 2 minutes. Drain and place the beans in the ice water. Drain.

Peel the inner skin from the fava beans.

Place the potatoes, onion, garlic, milk, and thyme in the pot and bring to a boil. Cook until the potatoes and onions are tender, about 15 to 20 minutes.

Place the potato mixture and the fava beans in a blender and blend until very smooth. If necessary, add a small amount of water.

Serve immediately, garnished with the thyme leaves and Parmesan cheese.

GARLIC-ROASTED RADICCHIO

I am not a fan of raw radicchio, but I like it roasted, which brings out its better bitter qualities. I learned to cook radicchio this way while in Italy. Be sure to cook the radicchio until it's fully crisped. Serve with Free-Form Tuscan-Style Rabbit Lasagna (page 224) or Simple Roasted Chicken (page 244).

SERVES 6 TO 8

8 garlic cloves, finely chopped
¼ cup olive oil
1 tablespoon chopped fresh rosemary leaves
¼ cup balsamic vinegar
1 teaspoon kosher salt
½ teaspoon black pepper
4 large heads radicchio, halved through the root
Grated Parmesan cheese, for garnish

Place the garlic, olive oil, rosemary, vinegar, salt, and pepper in a large bowl and mix well. Add the radicchio and gently toss so that it is well coated. Cover and let marinate at room temperature for at least 1 hour.

Preheat the oven to 425 degrees.

Place the radicchio in a baking pan and pour the marinade on top. Place in the oven and roast until the edges of the radicchio are crisp and almost beginning to look burnt, about 20 to 25 minutes.

Serve immediately, with grated Parmesan cheese.

GRILLED PORTOBELLO MUSHROOMS WITH TOMATO SAUCE

I call this recipe "the mushroom steak" because when portobellos are prepared this way, if you close your eyes, you'd swear you were eating steak. When you grill the mushrooms, think steak: you want the outside charred and the inside creamy and tender.

The great quality and flavor of portobello mushrooms makes them extremely popular at Olives. We go through many cases each week. In fact, we spend more money on portobello mushrooms than on any other vegetable.

Serve with pasta, Everyday Polenta (page 180), or Toasted Corn Polenta (page 188).

SERVES 4 TO 6

2 medium-size portobello mushrooms, stems removed, wiped clean
1 tablespoon olive oil
1 teaspoon kosher salt
1 teaspoon black pepper

TOMATO SAUCE:
2 tablespoons extra-virgin olive oil
3 to 4 garlic cloves, thinly sliced
5 plum tomatoes, fresh or canned, cut into small dice
1 teaspoon kosher salt
¼ teaspoon black pepper
⅓ cup dry white wine
½ cup water, Chicken Broth (page 38), or canned low-sodium
    chicken broth
6 fresh basil leaves, cut into slivers
Shaved Parmesan cheese for garnish (optional)

Prepare the grill or preheat the broiler.

Brush the mushrooms with the oil and sprinkle with the salt and pepper. Place them in a broiler pan or on a grill and cook until they are deeply browned, about 4 minutes per side. Remove from the heat. When the mushrooms are cool enough to handle, thinly slice them on an angle and set aside.

To make the tomato sauce: Place a medium-size skillet over medium-high heat and when it is hot, add the oil. Add the garlic and cook until it is golden and lightly toasted, about 2 to 3 minutes. Add the tomatoes, salt, and pepper and cook until the tomatoes are soft and stew-like, about 4 to 5 minutes. Add the wine and cook for 5 minutes. Add the broth and cook until the liquid has reduced by half, about 5 minutes more. Add the reserved mushrooms and the basil and cook until the mushrooms are warmed through, about 1 minute. Serve plain or with shaved Parmesan cheese over pasta or polenta.

My Mama's Zucchini

*O*ne of my strongest childhood memories is of eating this dish. It seemed as if we ate this daily in the summer, because we always had tons of zucchini in the garden. Mom claims that she didn't use mint, but I'm sure she did. Now, when I've been traveling a lot, I always come home to a house that smells of stewed zucchini, because Olivia knows that this dish means "home" to me.

This can be served on its own as a side dish or over pasta or polenta for an entrée. For an even heartier meal, add one to two cups of white cannellini beans just before adding the garnishes and cook until heated through.

SERVES 6 TO 8

2 tablespoons olive oil
2 anchovy fillets, chopped
1 Spanish onion, chopped
4 to 5 garlic cloves, thinly sliced
2 Idaho potatoes, peeled and cut into thick slices
4 medium-size zucchini, cut into thick slices
2 cups canned or fresh tomatoes, coarsely chopped
½ cup dry white wine
1 generous tablespoon chopped fresh oregano leaves or 1 teaspoon dried
  oregano, preferably Greek
1 teaspoon kosher salt
½ teaspoon black pepper
½ teaspoon crushed red pepper flakes
2 tablespoons chopped fresh flat-leaf parsley leaves, for garnish
Shaved Parmesan cheese, for garnish
1 tablespoon chopped fresh mint, for garnish (optional)

Place a large cast-iron skillet over medium-high heat and when it is hot, add the oil. Add the anchovy fillets, onion, and garlic, and stir well.

Cook until the onions are slightly browned and crisp on the edges, about 4 to 6 minutes. Add the potatoes and zucchini and cook until they are lightly browned, about 10 minutes.

Stir in the tomatoes and add the wine, oregano, salt, black pepper, and red pepper flakes. Reduce the heat to medium-low and cook at a low simmer until the zucchini is soft but still holds it shape, about 45 minutes.

Garnish with the parsley, Parmesan cheese, and, if desired, the mint.

Olivia and Simon, Isabelle, and Oliver English

ROASTED CUMIN CARROTS

These carrots were inspired by some of the *mezze* (appetizers) I ate while in Israel. The combination of the carrots, feta cheese, and cumin produces a dish that is surprisingly rich in flavor. At Olives, my favorite way to serve this is as part of an antipasto platter. It's also an excellent accompaniment to Tahini-Marinated Chicken (page 230) or Barbecued Shrimp with Chorizo Sauce (page 312). You can substitute almost any root vegetable, such as potatoes, parsnips, turnips, or rutabagas, for the carrots.

SERVES 4 TO 6

3 pounds carrots, peeled and cut into large chunks
2 tablespoons olive oil
2 tablespoons ground cumin
2 teaspoons kosher salt
1 teaspoon black pepper
¼ cup chopped fresh cilantro leaves, plus additional for garnish
3 garlic cloves, finely chopped
½ cup crumbled feta cheese

Preheat the oven to 400 degrees.

Place all the ingredients except the feta in a large bowl and mix well. Spread on a large ungreased baking sheet. Roast until the carrots are soft inside and crisp and browned on the outside, about 45 minutes to 1 hour.

Add the feta cheese, toss gently, and garnish with the cilantro. Serve hot or at room temperature.

BROCCOLI RABE WITH SAUSAGE

$\mathcal{I}$'m a broccoli rabe freak. I love it cooked almost any way.

The success of this dish is dependent on the proper toasting of the anchovies and the garlic. Sauté them well but not to the point of bitterness. The sausage is not absolutely necessary, but it makes a dish with more depth than your average sautéed broccoli rabe. Serve alone or over rigatoni or Everyday Polenta (page 180).

SERVES 4

1 bunch broccoli rabe, trimmed and well washed
3 sweet Italian sausages (about 12 ounces) (optional)
1 tablespoon olive oil
2 anchovy fillets, finely minced
4 shallots, thinly sliced
4 garlic cloves, thinly sliced
1 teaspoon kosher salt
½ teaspoon black pepper
¼ teaspoon crushed red pepper flakes (optional)
3 to 4 tablespoons water
Shaved or grated Parmesan cheese, for garnish

Place the broccoli rabe in a large skillet with 2 inches of water and bring to a boil over high heat. Cover and cook until the broccoli rabe is soft and wilted, about 7 to 10 minutes. Drain and set aside.

Wipe the skillet clean and place it over medium-high heat. When it is hot, add the sausages. Cook until the sausages are browned and thoroughly cooked, about 10 minutes. Drain the sausages on paper towels. Discard the fat and wipe the pan clean. When the sausages are cool enough to handle, cut into medium dice.

Reheat the skillet and add the oil. Add the anchovies, shallots, and garlic, stirring well after each addition, and cook until they are golden and lightly toasted, about 2 to 3 minutes. Add the reserved sausage and broccoli rabe, the salt, pepper, crushed red pepper flakes, if desired, and water and simmer for 5 minutes. Serve immediately, garnished with Parmesan cheese.

WHOLE ROASTED CAULIFLOWER WITH HONEY-AND-SPICE RUB

$\mathcal{F}$or cauliflower haters, this will be a revelation. It looks like a little roasted chicken. And the taste? Peppery. Sweet. Crunchy and soft.

SERVES 4

HONEY-AND-SPICE RUB:
½ cup honey
½ teaspoon ground coriander
2 tablespoons finely chopped peeled fresh ginger or 2 teaspoons
  ground ginger
1 tablespoon fresh lemon juice
2 bay leaves, crumbled
1 teaspoon toasted sesame oil
½ teaspoon kosher salt
1 teaspoon black pepper

1 head cauliflower, leaves intact
½ to 1 cup water

Preheat the oven to 400 degrees.

To make the rub: Place the honey, coriander, ginger, lemon juice, bay leaves, sesame oil, salt, and pepper in a small bowl and mix together until well combined. Set aside.

Place the cauliflower, leafy side down, in a baking pan just big enough to hold it snugly, and drizzle the rub over it. Place the cauliflower in the oven and bake until it is golden brown, about 1 hour. Add ½ cup water to the pan, and cook until the cauliflower is well browned and soft, about another 30 minutes. Check occasionally to see if the water has evaporated, and if necessary, add more water.

Remove the cauliflower and slice it. Pour the cooking liquid over the cauliflower and serve.

BRAISED ENDIVE WITH MORELS

I'm a big fan of raw endive but I also love to eat it cooked. Cooking the endive completely changes its character. Instead of crunchy and refreshing, its texture becomes rich and meaty.

SERVES 4 TO 6

■ *When Massachusetts was going through a moderate recession, local farmers complained about the prices they were getting for their crops. Our then-governor, Michael Dukakis, listened to their plight and countered, "Maybe you should grow endive or something." It became a huge joke in the local press, but I thought it was one of the more intelligent things he ever said. I may be giving him more credit than is due, but I'd like to think he had the foresight to see that a food revolution was stewing and that the farmers were going to have to diversify.*

5 to 6 dried morels
4 cups Chicken Broth (page 38) or canned low-sodium chicken broth
2 tablespoons olive oil
3 large Belgian endives, halved through the root
1 teaspoon kosher salt
1 teaspoon black pepper
⅔ cup chopped slab bacon or chopped high-quality thick-sliced lean bacon
3 shallots, thinly sliced
2 garlic cloves, thinly sliced
1 sprig fresh thyme
2 bay leaves, crumbled
2 tablespoons fresh lemon juice (about ½ lemon)

Place the morels in 1 cup of cold water, then drain well. Repeat two more times. Cover with hot water and let soak for 1 hour. Remove the morels from the water and carefully pour the top half to one-third of the liquid into another bowl. Discard the remainder.

Place the morels, the morel soaking liquid, and the chicken broth in a medium saucepan over high heat and bring to a boil. Reduce the heat to low and simmer until the morels are soft, about 10 minutes. Remove the morels from the pan, reserving the liquid. When they are cool enough to handle, chop the morels and return them to the cooking liquid; set aside.

Place a large skillet over medium-low heat and when it is hot, add the oil. Add the endives, cut side down, and sprinkle with the salt and pepper. Cook until the endives begin to brown, about 5 minutes. Add the bacon, shallots, and garlic, stirring well after each addition, and cook until the endives are caramelized, about 5 minutes.

Add the thyme, the bay leaves, and the reserved broth and morels and bring to a low boil. Reduce the heat to low and cook until the endives are very tender, about 45 minutes. Add the lemon juice and serve immediately.

EGGPLANT CAPONATA

I've taken a great classic dish and embellished it with some unexpected but harmonious ingredients. If you can, make this the day before you need it. It tastes even better the second day.

For a great luncheon dish, serve this on bread, or serve it as a dinner accompaniment to Simple Roasted Chicken (page 244) or grilled swordfish.

■ *Intense lemony capers are the brined flower buds of a bush found only in the Mediterranean area. Be sure to rinse them before using.*

■ *It has been said that Arabs discovered eggplant in India four thousand years ago and that Thomas Jefferson brought the first seeds to America. Eggplants change completely to reflect the technique used to cook them and the flavors they are combined with. The best eggplants are firm, shiny, and heavy. Buy them just prior to using, as they do not store well: an old eggplant will be very bitter. Most people are familiar with the oval deep-purple eggplant. I also like the large white round Sicilian variety.*

SERVES 4 TO 6

1 eggplant, peeled and cut into medium dice
1 tablespoon plus 1 teaspoon kosher salt
12 ounces sweet Italian sausage
2 tablespoons olive oil
1 small red onion, minced
3 garlic cloves, minced

½ cup golden raisins

1 teaspoon minced peeled fresh ginger

2 to 3 teaspoons chopped capers

1 cup chopped fresh or canned tomatoes

1 cup orange juice

1 tablespoon curry powder

¼ to ½ teaspoon crushed red pepper flakes

1 teaspoon honey

¼ to 1 cup water

2 tablespoons balsamic vinegar

3 tablespoons chopped fresh basil leaves

2 tablespoons chopped fresh cilantro leaves

2 tablespoons chopped fresh parsley leaves

1 tablespoon chopped fresh rosemary leaves

2 tablespoons chopped scallions

Sprinkle the eggplant with 1 tablespoon of the kosher salt. Place a large nonstick pan over medium heat and when it is hot, add the eggplant. Cook until the eggplant is golden brown on all sides, about 10 to 15 minutes. Remove the eggplant from the pan, drain on paper towels, and set it aside.

Reheat the pan. Add the sausage and cook over medium-high heat until golden brown and cooked through, about 7 minutes. Drain the sausage on paper towels. Discard the fat from the pan. When the sausage is cool enough to handle, roughly chop it.

Reheat the pan and add the oil. Add the onion and garlic and cook until the onion is softened, about 2 minutes. Add the reserved sausage, reserved eggplant, raisins, ginger, capers, tomatoes, orange juice, curry powder, pepper flakes, honey, and ¼ cup water, and the remaining 1 teaspoon salt, stirring well after each addition. Reduce the heat to medium-low and cook, adding a bit more water as needed, until the eggplant is soft and the mixture is chunky and has the consistency of a sauce, about 30 minutes.

Remove the pan from the heat and add the vinegar, basil, cilantro, parsley, rosemary, and scallions. Serve at room temperature.

ASH-ROASTED ARTICHOKES

*T*his recipe looks like a lot of work and time, but it's worth it. Don't worry about the artichokes overcooking; they longer they cook, the better they get.

SERVES 6

6 large artichokes, top ½ inch cut off and leaves and stem trimmed
12 garlic cloves, quartered
12 sprigs fresh mint
6 bay leaves
6 tablespoons honey
⅔ cup olive oil
1 teaspoon kosher salt
½ teaspoon black pepper

Prepare the grill or preheat the oven to 400 degrees. If you are using a grill, let the coals burn to ashes.

Open up the artichokes by placing both thumbs in the middle of each one and pulling the leaves apart. Fill each cavity with 2 garlic cloves, 2 sprigs of mint, 1 bay leaf, 1 tablespoon honey, and 1 to 2 tablespoons olive oil. Sprinkle with the salt and pepper.

If using a grill, bury the artichokes in the ashes just up to the top so that the tip of the artichoke is sticking out. If using an oven, place the artichokes directly on the oven rack. Cook until the artichokes are black on the outside, about 45 minutes to 1 hour.

Pull off the charred leaves and serve the heart.

■ *ARTICHOKE TALK*
One of my fondest memories of Italy is of attending an outdoor barbecue, which included whole roasted lamb and pig, antipasto, and my favorite, **carciofata,** *whole ash-roasted artichokes. We*

were in the Lazio region, just outside of Rome, an area where they grow vast amounts of artichokes; harvest is in the late spring to early summer. The whole process was amazing. They built a large bonfire and let it burn to ashes, then spread the ashes out in a large rectangular shape. Meanwhile, they painstakingly stuffed the center of the artichokes with mint and garlic cloves and poured what seemed to be about half a cup of the pure green local olive oil into the center of each one. The cooks then put on big heavy gloves, buried the globes in the ashes, and let them roast until the outsides were charred, roughly an hour and a half to two hours. When the artichokes were done, the cooks put the big heavy gloves back on and pulled the globes out. Then they pulled the leaves back, and the artichokes would be so soft that you could squeeze out the flesh of the heart. You mix the flesh with the mint, garlic, and olive oil, and add salt and pepper, and that's how you eat them, truly one of the greatest—if not the greatest—artichoke experiences I've ever had.

The artichokes you find in Italy have a heart that is much more tender than in the ones we have in the States, so you can eat more of it. Artichokes are harvested according to bulb size in this country, so you find different sizes and grades. I use the little ones (which are actually full grown) a lot because the choke is tender enough to eat and they have fewer tough outer leaves than the large ones, so the yield is bigger. When I want to use bottoms, I look for larger artichokes, because the bottom is much more meaty, although the choke is inedible. My favorite way to eat artichokes is steamed and served with a little melted butter or virgin olive oil and salt.

CREAMED SPINACH

Creamed spinach, which to me is *serious* comfort food, is one of those great classic dishes that you can't get in many restaurants (including my own). It's made with béchamel, the only classic sauce that I still use.

Creamed spinach is good with everything: toss it with any wide-cut noodle, mix it into your favorite risotto, or serve it on top of Everyday Polenta (page 180).

■ *I hate hearty, crinkle leaf cello spinach. I don't know who invented it, but I'm sure it was designed to be packed and shipped long distances. Cello spinach is why we all have bad memories of eating spinach. Use only leaf or bunch spinach (do not use cello spinach).*

MAKES 2½ TO 3 CUPS, SERVING 6

3 pounds leaf spinach, trimmed and well washed
½ teaspoon kosher salt
½ teaspoon black pepper

BÉCHAMEL SAUCE:
4 to 5 whole cloves
½ Spanish onion, chopped
3 cups milk
3 tablespoons unsalted butter
3 tablespoons all-purpose flour
1 teaspoon kosher salt
Pinch of white pepper
Pinch of ground nutmeg
2 tablespoons grated Parmesan cheese

Place 2 inches of water in a large pot and bring it to a boil over medium-high heat. Add the spinach, salt, and pepper and cook for 1 minute. Drain and rinse the leaves with very cold water. Drain well and set aside.

To make the béchamel: Insert the cloves into the onion. Place the milk in a small saucepan over medium heat and bring to a low boil. Add the onion and simmer for 5 minutes. Remove from the heat and discard the onion.

In a medium-size skillet, melt the butter over medium heat. Slowly whisk in the flour and cook until it has the consistency of mashed potatoes. Gradually add the milk, whisking all the while, and cook until the béchamel loses its floury taste, about 5 to 7 minutes. Add the salt and pepper.

Place the béchamel and spinach in a food processor fitted with a steel blade and pulse to blend. Gradually add the nutmeg and Parmesan cheese. Transfer back to the pan and reheat gently.

CREAMED SPINACH DUMPLINGS WITH TWO SAUCES

*B*ecause they are inexpensive to prepare and incredibly filling, almost every culture has a dumpling. These dumplings, essentially spinach gnocchi, are surprisingly light, like little cream puffs. Serve them with either or both sauces—as an appetizer or an accompaniment to a steak dinner (if you are making only one sauce, double the recipe).

SERVES 5 TO 6; MAKES ABOUT 30 DUMPLINGS

2 cups Creamed Spinach (page 154)
1½ cups all-purpose flour
5 large eggs
1 teaspoon kosher salt
2 tablespoons grated Parmesan cheese
Tomato Ragù and/or Brown Butter (recipes follow)

Place the creamed spinach, flour, eggs, salt, and cheese in a large mixing bowl and mix until thoroughly combined.

Bring a large pot of water to a boil over high heat. Drop heaping tablespoons of the spinach mixture into the water. After the dumplings come to the surface, allow them to simmer for an additional 2 minutes. Remove them with a slotted spoon and serve on top of the ragù or with the brown butter.

TOMATO RAGÙ

2 tablespoons olive oil
½ Spanish onion, chopped
1 heaping tablespoon chopped garlic

8 plum tomatoes, chopped
6 to 8 fresh basil leaves, chopped
2 tablespoons water

Place a large skillet over medium-high heat and when it is hot, add the oil. Add the onion and garlic and cook until golden, about 2 minutes. Add the tomatoes, basil, and water and cook until the ragù has thickened somewhat, about 12 to 15 minutes.

BROWN BUTTER

4 tablespoons unsalted butter
Juice of 1 lemon
Shaved or grated Parmesan cheese

Place the butter in a medium-size saucepan and cook over medium-high heat until it has browned, about 3 minutes. Add 15 dumplings and stir. Add the lemon juice and transfer to a large serving platter. Sprinkle with Parmesan cheese.

STUFFED ZUCCHINI PANCAKES WITH CRABMEAT

*T*o me these pancakes are the epitome of summer tastes: fresh-picked zucchini and crabmeat. Although they can be served alone, I like to use them as a garnish, usually for a simple grilled fish, such as snapper or swordfish. Serve these with Walnut Romesco (page 47), Citrus Aïoli (page 36), or Spicy Aïoli (page 35).

SERVES 6; MAKES 10 TO 12 PANCAKES

3 zucchini, julienned (by hand or with a Japanese mandoline)
3 large eggs
2 cups fine fresh bread crumbs
1½ teaspoons kosher salt
1½ teaspoons black pepper
8 ounces fresh cooked crabmeat, picked over
1 tablespoon grated peeled fresh ginger
1 tablespoon chopped fresh thyme leaves
1 tablespoon grainy mustard
2 tablespoons sour cream
1 tablespoon sherry vinegar
2 tablespoons olive oil

Place the zucchini, eggs, bread crumbs, 1 teaspoon of the salt, and 1 teaspoon of the pepper in a large bowl and mix thoroughly.

Place the crabmeat, ginger, thyme, mustard, sour cream, vinegar, and the remaining ½ teaspoon salt and ½ teaspoon pepper in a large bowl and mix gently.

Place a large cast-iron skillet over medium heat and when it is hot, add the oil. Drop heaping tablespoons of the zucchini mixture into the pan, pressing each one down lightly with the back of a spoon. Top each pancake with about 1 tablespoon of the crab mixture and then with another tablespoon of the zucchini mixture, pressing down lightly with the back of the spoon. Cook for about 4 minutes, turning once.

PORTOBELLO PICCATA WITH TWO SAUCES

*O*ne of my favorite things to eat is breaded boneless chicken. I've adapted the same breading technique to portobello mushrooms, and I ended up liking this version better than its inspiration.

You can also serve either sauce on top of grilled steak or chicken. These mushrooms make a great portobello sandwich with Parmesan cheese.

SERVES 4 AS AN ENTRÉE OR 8 AS AN APPETIZER

½ cup all-purpose flour
½ teaspoon kosher salt
¼ teaspoon black pepper
2 large eggs, lightly beaten
½ cup plain dry bread crumbs
1 tablespoon unsalted butter
1 tablespoon olive oil
8 medium-size portobello mushrooms, stems trimmed, mushrooms
*   wiped clean*
6 to 8 ounces fresh buffalo mozzarella cheese, cut into 8 slices
2 tablespoons chopped fresh basil leaves
Fresh Tomato Sauce and/or Lemon Sage Artichoke Sauce (recipes follow)

Preheat the oven to 350 degrees.

Combine the flour, salt, and pepper on a plate, place the eggs in a shallow bowl and spread the bread crumbs in another.

Place a large ovenproof skillet over medium-high heat and when it is hot, add the butter and oil. Dip the mushrooms in the flour, then the eggs, and then in the bread crumbs, add them to the skillet, and cook until they are browned, about 1 minute on each side.

Transfer the skillet to the oven and bake for 10 minutes.

Remove the skillet from the oven and arrange the mushrooms in an overlapping circle, with the slices of mozzarella between them. Sprinkle with the basil and return the skillet to the oven until the cheese melts, about 2 minutes. Serve with one or both sauces (if you are using only one of the sauces, double the recipe).

FRESH TOMATO SAUCE

3 tablespoons extra-virgin olive oil
3 garlic cloves, thinly sliced
1 large beefsteak tomato, diced
½ cup dry white wine
1 teaspoon kosher salt
½ teaspoon black pepper

Place a medium-size saucepan over medium-high heat and when it is hot, add the oil. Add the garlic and cook until it is lightly browned, about 3 minutes. Add the tomato, wine, salt, and pepper and cook until the liquid has reduced by one-fourth, about 10 minutes. Spoon onto a seving platter and top with the portobello piccata.

LEMON SAGE ARTICHOKE SAUCE

2 tablespoons unsalted butter
6 fresh, frozen, or canned artichoke bottoms, thinly sliced (see instructions
*   on page 67 for fresh artichokes)*
2 tablespoons chopped fresh flat-leaf parsley
6 fresh sage leaves, cut into slivers
3 tablespoons fresh lemon juice (about ¾ lemon)
Grated Parmesan cheese, for garnish

Melt the butter in a medium-size skillet over medium-high heat. Cook until it is browned, about 3 minutes. Add the artichoke bottoms, parsley, sage, and lemon juice, stirring well after each addition, and cook until artichokes are hot, about 2 minutes. Spoon onto a serving platter and top with the portobello piccata. Garnish with the Parmesan cheese.

POTATO DISHES ▪

BLACK TRUFFLE, POTATO, AND PARSNIP "RISOTTO"

*I*n this recipe I use the term *risotto* to describe the technique rather than the dish: the potatoes and parsnips are cut to the size of rice grains and then stirred gradually just as you do with risotto. This creates a sauce that binds them together with the truffle peelings.

I've always found that if you cook the foods that are grown together, you get real magic. Truffles, parsnips, and potatoes are all grown underground, and the recipe enhances their earthy, sensual taste.

Serve with any duck dish.

■ *Truffles cost at least $20 to $40 per ounce, so we're not expecting you to go out and buy a pound of fresh truffles. If you can find a shop that sells small amounts of fresh truffles, it's well worth the trouble and the expense to buy them. If you can't find fresh, you can use canned or frozen or purchase them by mail-order (page 351). When shopping for fresh truffles, be sure to note the pungency, which will vary from purveyor to purveyor, region to region, and year to year. Canned truffle peelings are available in gourmet and specialty stores and cost about $60 for a sixteen-ounce can. To make the most of your investment, make this dish the same week you make Spaghetti with Truffle Mascarpone (page 220). Freeze the rest of the truffles.*

SERVES 6

1 tablespoon olive oil

½ Spanish onion, cut into very small dice

2 medium Idaho potatoes, peeled and cut into very small dice (a little larger than a grain of rice)

1 small parsnip, peeled and cut into very small dice

4 to 4½ cups Chicken Broth (page 38), canned low-sodium chicken broth, or water

1 to 2 tablespoons fresh, frozen, or canned black truffle peelings

2 teaspoons kosher salt

1 teaspoon black pepper

¾ teaspoon truffle oil (see page 351) (optional)

½ cup grated Parmesan cheese

2 to 4 tablespoons unsalted butter, at room temperature (optional)

½ cup chopped fresh flat-leaf parsley leaves, for garnish

Place a large saucepan over medium-low heat and when it is hot, add the oil. Add the onion and cook until it is translucent, about 3 minutes. Add the potatoes, parsnip, broth, and truffle peelings and bring to a boil. Reduce the heat to low and cook, uncovered, at a gentle boil for 20 minutes.

Add the salt, pepper, and the truffle oil, if desired, and continue cooking until all the liquid has been absorbed by the vegetables, about 10 minutes. Remove the pan from the heat and stir in the Parmesan cheese and, if desired, the butter. Garnish with the parsley. Serve immediately.

My Favorite Baked Potato Salad

*O*n Sunday nights when Olives is closed and I've had a long, hectic week, I sometimes just can't bear the thought of dirtying any pots and pans. I throw some potatoes in the oven, pop open some Sangiovese or Chianti, and hang out with Olivia, Oliver, Isabelle, and Simon while the potatoes roast.

If you have a fireplace, try wrapping the potatoes in foil and cooking them in the ashes. When you open the potatoes, first let the steam escape and then plop the salad right on top.

SERVES 4

4 Idaho potatoes, pricked several times with the tines of a fork

1 tablespoon olive oil

1 teaspoon kosher salt

1 teaspoon black pepper

*1 small bunch watercress, well washed, dried, and torn into
       bite-size pieces*

1 cucumber, peeled and thinly sliced

*1½ cups green beans, blanched in boiling salted water for 2 minutes and
       halved lengthwise*

1 small red onion, thinly sliced

1 Belgian endive, thinly sliced on the diagonal

DRESSING:

2 tablespoons extra-virgin olive oil

⅓ cup chopped walnuts

2 tablespoons fresh lemon juice (about ½ lemon)

2 tablespoons balsamic vinegar

¾ cup crumbled Roquefort, Maytag Blue, or other good-quality blue cheese

Preheat the oven to 400 degrees.

Rub the potatoes with the olive oil, ½ teaspoon of the salt, and ½ teaspoon of the pepper, place them directly on a rack in the oven, and cook until tender, about 40 minutes to 1 hour, depending on the size of the potatoes.

Meanwhile, to make the salad: Combine the watercress, cucumber, green beans, red onion, endive, and the remaining ½ teaspoon each salt and pepper in a large mixing bowl.

To make the dressing: Place a small skillet over high heat and when it is hot, add the oil. Add the walnuts and toast for 2 minutes. Add the lemon juice and vinegar and cook until heated through, about 1 minute. Take the pan off the heat and add the cheese. Pour the dressing over the vegetables and mix to combine.

Open the potatoes by making a large "X" on the top of each one and squeezing open with your hands. Mound one quarter of the salad into and on each hot potato. Serve immediately.

LACY POTATO PANCAKE WITH LEEKS, GOAT CHEESE, AND APPLE RAGÙ

*T*his is a wonderful and sophisticated dish that's perfect for both adults and children. Serve it at a brunch where you're feeding all ages. This is especially good with pork or venison.

SERVES 4

APPLE RAGÙ:
1 teaspoon olive oil
3 Cortland apples, peeled, cored, and thickly sliced
1 cup apple cider
1 generous tablespoon dry sherry
Juice of 1 lemon
1 tablespoon chopped peeled fresh ginger
2 tablespoons Dijon mustard
¼ cup chopped scallion greens
Pinch of cayenne pepper

2 Idaho potatoes, cut into matchstick slices (with a Japanese mandoline or by hand)
1 leek (white and tender green part), well washed and julienned
1 teaspoon kosher salt
1 teaspoon black pepper
¼ cup olive oil
½ cup crumbled goat cheese

To make the apple ragù: Place a large nonstick skillet over medium-high heat and when it is hot, add the oil. Add the apples and cook until they caramelize slightly, about 5 minutes. Add the apple cider, stir, and bring to a low boil. Add the sherry, lemon juice, and ginger and cook until the apples are soft, about 15 minutes. Off the heat, add the scallions and cayenne and set aside.

Combine the potatoes, leeks, salt, and pepper in a small bowl.

Place a medium-size nonstick skillet over medium heat and when it is hot, add the oil. Add half the potato mixture and pat down to form a pancake. Cook until it is lightly browned on the underside. Remove and drain on a paper towel. Repeat with the remaining potato mixture, but do not remove the pancake from the pan when it is cooked. Dot it with the goat cheese, place the other pancake on top, and press down gently. Cook until the cheese has melted, about 2 to 3 minutes.

Cut the potato pancake in quarters and serve topped with apple ragù.

Apple-Fennel Mashed Potatoes

*I*t has been said that I followed the mashed potato wave to fame and I can't really argue. The natural combination of the apples and potatoes (*pomme de terre*, French for potatoes, means "apples of the earth"), works perfectly together, and the fennel adds just the right amount of zing. Serve with Gingered Slow-Braised Lamb Shanks (page 272).

You can make this dish without the cream and reheat it the next day.

SERVES 6

½ cup chopped slab bacon or chopped thick-sliced high-quality lean bacon,
    or 1 tablespoon olive oil

1 fennel bulb, trimmed, cored, and cut into large dice

3 Idaho potatoes, peeled and cut into large dice

1 cooking apple, such as McIntosh, Granny Smith, Cortland, or Winesap,
    peeled and chopped (about 1½ cups)

1 tablespoon chopped fresh rosemary leaves

3½ cups water

1 cup apple cider

¼ to ½ cup light or heavy cream

1 teaspoon Pernod

1 tablespoon unsalted butter, at room temperature

2 scallions, chopped

1 teaspoon kosher salt

1 teaspoon black pepper

If using the bacon, place a large saucepan over medium-high heat and when it is hot, add the bacon. Cook for 2 minutes, then drain off the rendered fat. If you are not using bacon, add the oil to the hot pan. Add the fennel and cook for 2 minutes. Add the potatoes and cook for 1 minute. Add the apple, rosemary, water, and apple cider and bring to a boil. Reduce the heat to medium and cook, uncovered, until the potatoes are tender, about 35 minutes.

Add the cream and cook for 5 minutes.

Remove the pan from the heat and mash the ingredients. Add the Pernod, butter, scallions, salt, and pepper. Serve immediately.

CHORIZO MASHED POTATOES WITH SCALLION CREAM

There is a very large Portuguese community in Boston, serviced by small markets that sell Portuguese products rarely seen in larger grocery stores. They sell a kind of chorizo (*chorizo* means "sausage" in Portuguese) that is hot and smoky, but I'm sure nothing like it is seen in Portugal.

At Olives, we serve the potatoes as the recipe indicates, but those with less hefty appetites might want to reduce the cream to one cup. You won't want to serve this every day because it's more like a newfangled hash than mashed potatoes, and unbelievably rich. (Just don't hold me responsible when your doctor lectures you about cholesterol.)

Serve with Grilled Molasses-Cured Tuna (page 295).

■ *For a change, you could make twice-baked potatoes: Roast the potatoes and scoop out the flesh. Mix it with the remaining ingredients and then stuff it all back in the skin. Bake until heated through, about 20 minutes.*

■ *Chorizo, or chouriço, is a spicy cured sausage that is used primarily in Spanish and Portuguese cooking. It can range from mild to hot and is generally made from pork meat, pork fat, scallions, garlic, paprika, salt, vinegar, and spices. Linguiça is a milder version. Both can readily be found in many grocery stores and in markets that stock Latin American products. It can also be mail-ordered (page 351).*

SERVES 6 TO 8

2 pounds Idaho potatoes, unpeeled, diced
1 bunch scallions, chopped
2 cups heavy cream
1 heaping tablespoon chopped fresh rosemary leaves or 1 teaspoon
    dried rosemary
2 cups chopped fresh chorizo sausage (about 12 ounces)
3 garlic cloves, thinly sliced
1 tablespoon unsalted butter
2 teaspoons kosher salt
1 teaspoon black pepper

Place the potatoes in a large saucepan, cover with cold water, and bring to a boil over high heat. Reduce the heat to medium and cook until the potatoes are tender, about 15 minutes. Drain and return the potatoes to the saucepan.

Meanwhile, place the scallions, cream, and rosemary in a blender and blend until thickened and creamy. Set aside.

Place a skillet over medium-high heat and add the chorizo, garlic, and butter. Cook until the chorizo has caramelized and become brown and crispy, about 5 minutes.

Mash the potatoes with a fork or potato masher, then gradually incorporate the scallion cream and the chorizo. Cook over low heat until the liquid has been absorbed, about 3 minutes. Add the salt and pepper and serve immediately.

COUNTRY WALNUT MASHED POTATOES

*Y*et another mashed potato recipe. I always joke with my cooking staff that one day I'll open up the Baskin-Robbins of mashed potatoes—at least thirty-one flavors.

Try this topped with Roquefort or blue cheese and serve with steak or Simple Roasted Chicken (page 244). Or omit the cheese and serve it with grilled salmon.

SERVES 4

4 large Red Bliss or Yukon Gold potatoes (about 1½ to 2 pounds),
unpeeled, cut into large dice
1 tablespoon unsalted butter
½ cup coarsely chopped walnuts
¼ to ½ cup sour cream
1 teaspoon kosher salt
½ teaspoon black pepper
1 tablespoon grated Parmesan cheese

Place the potatoes in a large saucepan, cover with cold water, and bring to a boil over high heat. Reduce the heat to medium and cook until the potatoes are tender, about 15 minutes. Drain and return to the pot. Mash with a fork or potato masher.

While the potatoes are cooking, place a small skillet over medium-high heat and when it is hot, add the butter. Add the walnuts and cook until they are lightly toasted.

Add the walnuts, sour cream, salt, pepper, and Parmesan to the potatoes and mix well. If necessary, reheat over low heat. Serve immediately.

GARLIC MASHED POTATOES

*R*ich and creamy, these are the perfect mashed potatoes, and they go with everything.

SERVES 4

2 pounds new potatoes, unpeeled, cut into large dice
1 tablespoon unsalted butter
4 to 5 garlic cloves, crushed
2 cups heavy cream
1 teaspoon kosher salt
½ teaspoon black pepper

Place the potatoes in a large saucepan, cover with cold water, and bring to a boil over high heat. Reduce the heat to medium and cook until the potatoes are tender, about 15 minutes. Drain and return to the pot. Mash with a fork or potato masher.

While the potatoes are cooking, melt the butter in a small skillet over medium-high heat. Add the garlic and cook until the garlic is just golden, 2 to 3 minutes. Add the cream and cook until it has reduced by half, about 7 minutes. Add the garlic cream, salt, and pepper to the potatoes and mix well. If necessary, reheat over low heat. Serve immediately.

CARROT MASHED POTATOES

*M*uch lighter and sweeter than any of the other mashed potatoes. I once served this to my then-baby-daughter, Isabelle, who promptly ate three servings for breakfast.

SERVES 4 TO 6

1 tablespoon unsalted butter
1 tablespoon finely chopped peeled fresh ginger
2 garlic cloves, finely chopped
1½ pounds carrots, peeled, halved lengthwise, and each half cut
    into quarters
2 Idaho potatoes, peeled and cut into large dice
¼ teaspoon ground nutmeg
1 teaspoon kosher salt
½ teaspoon black pepper
¼ cup sour cream or plain yogurt
2 tablespoons maple syrup

Place the carrots and potatoes in a large saucepan, cover with cold water, and bring to a boil over high heat. Reduce the heat to medium and cook until tender, about 20 minutes. Drain and place in a medium-size mixing bowl.

While the carrots and potatoes are cooking, melt the butter in a small skillet over medium heat. Add the ginger and garlic and cook until they are just golden, about 2 minutes.

Mash the potatoes and carrots with a fork or potato masher, gradually incorporating the garlic-and-ginger mixture, then the nutmeg, salt, pepper, sour cream, and maple syrup. Serve immediately.

MASHED SWEET POTATOES WITH MAPLE SYRUP

*T*hese definitely belong at the Thanksgiving table, but I serve them all year round.

SERVES 4 TO 6

3 large or 4 medium sweet potatoes, peeled and cubed
1 tablespoon chopped peeled fresh ginger
½ cup maple syrup
½ cup heavy cream
3 tablespoons unsalted butter, at room temperature
1 teaspoon kosher salt
½ teaspoon black pepper

Place the sweet potatoes in a large saucepan, cover with cold water, and bring to a boil over high heat. Reduce the heat to medium and cook until the potatoes are tender, about 20 minutes. Drain and transfer to a plate.

Add the ginger, maple syrup, and cream to the pot and bring to a boil over medium heat. Cook until the mixture is like thick caramel.

Return the potatoes to the saucepan and mash with a fork or potato masher, gradually incorporating the caramel mixture. Add the butter, salt, and pepper. Serve immediately.

Mashed Potato Cake

$\mathcal{T}$he perfect use for leftover mashed potatoes. It's a wonderful snack, or you could serve these as an accompaniment to grilled or roasted poultry or meat. The proportions of this recipe make one cake. Repeat the process to use all the leftover potatoes.

MAKES 1 POTATO CAKE, SERVING 1

1 tablespoon olive oil
⅔ cup Apple-Fennel Mashed Potatoes (page 170),
    Country Walnut Mashed Potatoes (page 174),
    or Carrot Mashed Potatoes (page 176), formed into a patty

Place a large cast-iron skillet over medium-high heat and when it is hot, add the oil. Place the patty in the skillet and cook until golden brown, about 5 to 7 minutes per side. Serve immediately.

POLENTA ▪

EVERYDAY POLENTA

*Y*our basic polenta—water, salt, and cornmeal—just doesn't do it for me. Here's our way to make polenta stand on its own. At Olives, we call this Everyday Polenta because it's always on the menu, but you won't want to eat it every day: it's simply too rich.

Jazz this up by topping it with a dollop of Eggplant Caponata, or serve it with Grilled Portobello Mushrooms with Tomato Sauce (page 138), Osso Buco of Veal (page 264), or Gingered Slow-Braised Lamb Shanks (page 272).

■ *Cornmeal that has been steel-ground has no husk, or flavor. Always use the more nutritious stone-ground cornmeal, which can be found in specialty and health food stores. Keep it in a cold place for no more than two months; it goes rancid very fast.*

SERVES 6 TO 8

8 cups water
2 teaspoons kosher salt
2 cups stone-ground yellow cornmeal
4 tablespoons unsalted butter, at room temperature
1 cup light or heavy cream
½ cup grated Parmesan cheese
½ cup grated Romano cheese
½ teaspoon black pepper, or more to taste

Place the water and salt in a medium-size saucepan and bring to a boil over high heat. Gradually pour in the cornmeal, whisking all the while. When the mixture begins to bubble, reduce the heat to medium-low and cook, stirring, until the cornmeal begins to thicken, about 10 to 15 minutes.

Slowly whisk in the remaining ingredients. Continue cooking until the polenta just begins to pull away from the sides of the pan, about 3 to 5 minutes. Serve immediately or follow the suggestions in "Polenta Talk," below.

■ *POLENTA TALK*

Polenta can be served soft as soon as it is ready, mashed potato–style, or cooled on a plate or baking sheet until firm, cut into squares or triangles, and then panfried or grilled.

To panfry, place a large skillet over medium-high heat and when it is hot, add a small amount of olive oil. Add the polenta and fry until golden, about 2 minutes per side.

To grill, brush with olive oil and grill until golden, about 2 minutes per side. You can also make great croutons with any leftover polenta. Cut the polenta into 2-inch cubes and then simply toss the cube with a small amount of olive oil. Place in a preheated 450-degree oven and bake until the cubes are lightly browned, about 5 to 7 minutes.

■ *PLACIDO*

My Uncle Placido was a master pastry chef from Venice who had been trained in Paris. He and Aunt Mary owned a small bakery in the Bronx. Whenever we were in New York, we would go to their house for Sunday dinner. Mary always prepared traditional family fare that her mother, Bettina, had taught her. Placido made the polenta, which he seemed to stir for hours and hours.

I never saw anyone else make polenta until I went to Italy in 1984. There cornmeal mush had been transformed from an everyday staple, eaten because there was nothing else, to haute cuisine, served with the most expensive cuts of meat and fish. For my taste buds, classic polenta is too bland, so the recipes that follow, while inspired by the traditional method, are not traditional in flavor.

FIG POLENTA WITH FRESH FIG SAUCE

I love adding fruits to polenta. This sauce is sweet and creamy and works particularly well with rich dishes like Olives Dry-Rubbed Roast Duck (page 248) and Pork Chops au Poivre (page 267).

SERVES 9

1 cup dried Black Mission figs, chopped
5 cups water
¼ cup lightly packed brown sugar
2 cups stone-ground yellow cornmeal
1 cup milk
4 tablespoons unsalted butter, at room temperature
½ cup grated Parmesan cheese
¼ to ½ cup chopped scallion greens
½ teaspoon kosher salt

15 fresh figs, halved
1 cup crumbled soft goat cheese, such as Montrachet
1 tablespoon chopped fresh rosemary leaves
¼ teaspoon kosher salt
¼ teaspoon black pepper
18 paper-thin slices prosciutto (optional)
2 cups frisée

Lightly butter an 8 x 8-inch baking pan.
Place the dried figs, water, and sugar in a medium-size saucepan and

bring to a rolling boil over high heat. Boil until the figs have plumped, about 5 minutes.

Gradually pour in the cornmeal, whisking all the while. When the mixture begins to bubble, reduce the heat to medium-low, gradually add the milk, and cook, stirring, until the cornmeal begins to thicken, about 10 to 15 minutes.

Slowly whisk in the butter, Parmesan cheese, scallions, and ½ teaspoon of the salt. Continue cooking until the polenta just begins to pull away from the sides of the pan, about 3 to 5 minutes.

Pour the polenta into the prepared pan and smooth it out so that it is an even thickness. Let cool to room temperature, cover, and refrigerate.

Preheat the oven to 350 degrees.

Cut the polenta into 9 squares. Transfer the pan to an ovenproof platter. Evenly distribute the fresh figs and goat cheese over the polenta squares. Sprinkle with the rosemary, the remaining ¼ teaspoon salt, and the pepper and place in the oven until the cheese has softened, about 7 to 10 minutes.

Top with the prosciutto, if desired, and surround with frisée.

HERB POLENTA

This is a somewhat leaner version of Everyday Polenta—minus the cream and Romano cheese but with the addition of fresh herbs. Use the suggested assortment or, if you prefer, use just one. Herb Polenta is great with just about anything, but it's particularly good with Bistro Stuffed Chicken (page 240), Roast Chicken with Herb and Lemon Paste (page 236), or Roasted Clams with Chicken, Tomatoes, Artichokes, and Bacon (page 314).

SERVES 6 TO 8

8 cups water
2 teaspoons kosher salt
2¼ cups stone-ground yellow cornmeal
¾ cup grated Parmesan cheese
4 tablespoons unsalted butter, at room temperature
¼ cup assorted chopped fresh herbs (rosemary, parsley, thyme, and/or
    oregano leaves)
½ teaspoon black pepper

Place the water and salt in a medium-size saucepan and bring to a boil over high heat. Gradually pour in the cornmeal, whisking all the while. When the mixture begins to bubble, reduce the heat to medium-low and cook, stirring, until the cornmeal begins to thicken, about 10 to 15 minutes.

Slowly whisk in the remaining ingredients. Continue cooking until the polenta just begins to pull away from the sides of the pan, about 3 to 5 minutes.

Serve immediately, or follow the suggestions in "Polenta Talk," page 181.

GOLDEN RAISIN POLENTA

*T*his is my favorite polenta; I can eat it right out of the pan almost any time of day. For brunch, serve it with pan-griddled smoked ham and for dinner, with Pork Chops au Poivre (page 267), Chicken Glazed in a Rhubarb Agrodolce (page 242), or Almond-Crusted Snapper (page 319). The sweetness of the raisins creates a contrast with the smokiness of the meats that makes it especially good served with bitter greens, such as broccoli rabe.

Feel free to substitute dark raisins, prunes, or currants for the golden raisins.

SERVES 4 TO 6

2 cups golden raisins
5 cups water
½ small white onion, chopped
1 cup stone-ground yellow cornmeal
1 teaspoon kosher salt
½ teaspoon black pepper
2 tablespoons unsalted butter, at room temperature
½ cup light or heavy cream

Place the raisins, water, and onion in a medium-size saucepan and simmer over medium heat until the raisins are well plumped and the mixture has reduced somewhat, about 30 minutes.

Increase the heat to high and bring to a boil. Gradually pour in the cornmeal, salt, and pepper, whisking all the while.

When the mixture begins to bubble, reduce the heat to medium-low and cook until the cornmeal begins to thicken, about 10 to 15 minutes.

Slowly whisk in the butter and cream. Continue cooking until the polenta just begins to pull away from the sides of the pan, about 3 to 5 minutes.

Serve immediately, or follow the serving suggestions in "Polenta Talk," page 181.

TOASTED CORN POLENTA
WITH FONTINA CHEESE

*T*oasting the corn caramelizes the sugar in it and gives it a nice nutty taste, adding a sweet, smoky dimension to the flavor. Serve this with Whole Roasted Rack of Veal (page 263), Simple Roasted Chicken (page 244), or Roast Chicken with Herb and Lemon Paste (page 236).

SERVES 6 TO 8

2 tablespoons olive oil
2 cups fresh corn kernels
4 cups water or Corn Stock (page 44)
1 teaspoon kosher salt
1 cup stone-ground yellow cornmeal
1 tablespoon unsalted butter, at room temperature
¼ to ½ cup light or heavy cream
1 cup grated Fontina cheese

Place a large skillet over medium-high heat and when it is hot, add the oil. Add the corn kernels and cook until they are evenly browned and just beginning to caramelize, about 6 minutes. Set aside.

Place the water and salt in a medium-size saucepan and bring to a boil over high heat. Gradually pour in the cornmeal, whisking all the while. When the mixture begins to bubble, reduce the heat to medium-low and cook, stirring, until the cornmeal begins to thicken, about 10 to 15 minutes.

Slowly whisk in the butter, cream, Fontina cheese, and reserved toasted corn kernels. Continue cooking until the polenta just begins to pull away from the sides of the pan, about 3 to 5 minutes.

Serve immediately or follow the suggestions in "Polenta Talk" (page 181).

RISOTTO ∎

SAFFRON RISOTTO

*T*raditional Milanese saffron risotto is made with beef marrow, one of the few foods that I rarely cook with anymore, although I do love the richness it adds. I am constantly trying to tweak this dish, increasing or reducing the amount of saffron or adding different types and combinations of sausage, shellfish, tomatoes, and fennel. But this is the most luscious (and yet simple) preparation, so I always go back to it.

Remember to keep risotto on the runny side. It should be silken and creamy in texture with a slight crunch of the grain. Serve this with Osso Buco of Veal (page 264).

SERVES 6 TO 8 AS A SIDE DISH

1 to 3 tablespoons unsalted butter
1 Spanish onion, finely chopped
2 chorizo sausages, cut into small dice
3 garlic cloves, minced
1 tablespoon saffron threads
1 cup dry white wine
2 cups arborio rice
8 cups Chicken Broth (page 38) or canned low-sodium chicken broth
2 tablespoons chopped scallions
2 tablespoons chopped fresh cilantro leaves
¼ cup grated Parmesan cheese
1 teaspoon kosher salt
½ teaspoon black pepper

Melt 1 tablespoon butter in a large straight-sided nonreactive saucepan over medium heat. Add the onion, chorizo, and garlic, stirring well after each addition, and cook until golden, about 5 to 6 minutes. Add the wine and cook until it has almost completely evaporated, about 4 minutes. Add the rice and stir until it is well coated.

Add 1 cup of the broth, stir well, scraping the bottom and sides of the pan, and cook until it has been absorbed by the rice. Continue adding the broth, 1 cup at a time, stirring well after each addition, until the liquid has been absorbed, about 18 to 20 minutes.

Stir in the scallions, cilantro, Parmesan, salt, pepper, and, if desired, 2 tablespoons of butter. Serve immediately.

■ *RISOTTO TALK*

When I came back from Italy in 1985, I had a hard time giving away risotto. Michela Larson, owner of the former Michela's, kept telling me to be patient, but hell, I was twenty-five years old and didn't know what patience was. Whenever I did a cooking demonstration, I always cooked and preached the sermon of risotto. Michela's admonition was true and risotto is now more popular than ever, and rightly so. Nutritious, filling, heartwarming, and soulful, it is one of the most intelligent dishes ever created. Risotto's real appeal is that it is eminently flexible: once you have mastered the technique, you can create your own dish—and have dinner on the table in less than thirty minutes. All you are left with is one pot to clean, and even that can be left to soak while you linger over your last sips of wine.

Risotto's main ingredient, arborio rice, flourishes in Italy's Po Valley. There are four grades of arborio rice, which are determined by the size, consistency, and color of the grain: risotto comune, semifino, fino, and superfino. Superfino is most readily available in the United States: long, fat, and pearly white, it has the greatest ability to absorb flavors. Do not substitute other types of rice: nothing else has the same high starch content or will produce the same creamy texture.

Most people tell you that the stock must be hot when you add it to the rice. I disagree. The hot stock causes the rice to spatter, which has the potential to break the grains. The trick is to create a slow, low simmer that enables the grains to slowly absorb the room-temperature liquid. When you spoon it out, risotto should sink on the plate, run a bit, and then stop.

Asparagus Risotto with Ragù of Crazy Mushrooms, Porcini Cream, and White Truffles

$\mathcal{T}$his recipe may seem a little complicated, but the ambrosial results are worth the effort.

SERVES 4 AS AN ENTRÉE OR 6 TO 8 AS AN APPETIZER

RAGÙ:
1 tablespoon olive oil
2 cups thinly sliced button mushrooms
2 cups thinly sliced mushrooms, such as shiitakes or portobellos
1 tablespoon unsalted butter
2 shallots, finely minced
¼ cup brandy
2 cups Chicken Broth (page 38) or canned low-sodium chicken broth
½ teaspoon chopped fresh rosemary leaves
½ teaspoon kosher salt
¼ teaspoon black pepper

PORCINI CREAM:
1 tablespoon olive oil
2 tablespoons fresh, dried, or frozen porcini mushrooms (soaked, if dried)
2 shallots, finely minced
1 garlic clove, minced
¼ cup dry white wine
½ cup Chicken Broth (page 38) or canned low-sodium chicken broth
½ cup heavy cream

1 teaspoon chopped fresh mint leaves
½ teaspoon chopped fresh rosemary leaves

ASPARAGUS RISOTTO:
1 bunch asparagus, woody ends trimmed and peeled
6 to 8 cups Chicken Broth (page 38) or Dark Stock (page 40)
1 tablespoon olive oil
1 large Spanish onion, finely chopped
2½ cups arborio rice
1 cup dry white wine
2 cups grated Fontina cheese
¼ cup grated Parmesan cheese
½ teaspoon kosher salt
½ teaspoon black pepper
A few shavings of white truffles (optional)
A few drops of white truffle oil (optional)

Fill a large bowl with ice water.

To make the mushroom ragù: Place a skillet over medium-high heat and when it is hot, add the olive oil. Add the mushrooms and butter and cook until the mushrooms are lightly browned, about 5 to 6 minutes. Add the shallots and cook for 3 minutes. Add the brandy and flambé. Add the chicken broth and cook until it has reduced by half, about 15 minutes. Add the rosemary, salt, and pepper. Cover, set aside, and keep warm.

To make the porcini cream: Place a skillet over medium heat and when it is hot, add the oil. Add the porcini, shallot, and garlic and cook for 3 minutes. Add the white wine and cook until the pan is almost dry, about 3 minutes. Add the chicken broth and heavy cream and simmer until reduced by half. Transfer the porcini cream to a blender, add the mint and rosemary, and blend until smooth.

Bring a large pot of water to a boil over high heat. Add the asparagus and cook until it turns bright green, about 3 minutes. Immediately place the asparagus in the ice water. Drain. Cut off the top 2 inches of the asparagus and set these tips aside.

Place the asparagus stalks and 1 cup of the broth in a blender or a food processor fitted with a steel blade and process until smooth. Set the asparagus puree aside.

Place a large straight-sided nonreactive saucepan over medium heat and when the pan is hot, add the olive oil. Add the onion and cook until golden, about 5 minutes. Add the rice and stir until it is well coated. Add the wine, stir, scraping the bottom and sides of the pan, and cook until it has been absorbed by the rice.

Add 1 cup of the broth and cook, stirring constantly, until the liquid has been absorbed by the rice. Continue adding the broth, 1 cup at a time, stirring well after each addition, until all the liquid has been absorbed, about 18 to 20 minutes.

Stir in the reserved asparagus puree and asparagus tips and the Fontina cheese, Parmesan cheese, salt, and pepper.

Place the mushroom ragù on a large platter, spreading the mushrooms out to the sides, and then pour the risotto down the middle. Dollop the porcini cream around the ragù. Shave white truffles on top of the risotto and drizzle with white truffle oil, if desired, and serve immediately.

Smoky Ham Hock and Corn Risotto with Red Beans

When I was growing up in Atlanta, we rarely ate out. I have clear memories, however, of the restaurants we went to: a few haunts with great, inventive Southern cooks, which inspired many of my dishes—this one among them. Serve with fried chicken or Fried Oysters (page 64).

■ *I am a huge fan of cilantro, an herb that people tend to have strong feelings about, either intensely pro or intensely con. Cilantro is almost never used in Italian cooking, but it is often found in Latin American, Portuguese, Mexican, Middle Eastern, and Asian dishes. Also called Chinese parsley, cilantro looks like flat-leaf parsley except that it is usually a lighter green, with more feathery leaves. It is often displayed with the roots still intact.*

SERVES 4 AS AN ENTREÉ OR 6 TO 8 AS A SIDE DISH

1 Spanish onion, finely diced
2 to 3 garlic cloves, minced
1 ham hock
4 to 6 ears of corn, husked only
1 celery stalk, finely diced
1 carrot, finely diced
1 sprig fresh rosemary
1 sprig fresh thyme
9 cups Chicken Broth (page 38), canned low-sodium chicken broth,
*   or Corn Stock (page 44)*
1 tablespoon olive oil

2 cups arborio rice

1 cup dry white wine

2 tablespoons unsalted butter, at room temperature (optional)

1 cup cooked red kidney beans, rinsed

1 teaspoon kosher salt

½ teaspoon black pepper

¼ cup finely chopped fresh cilantro leaves

¼ cup finely chopped scallions

¼ cup grated Parmesan cheese, or more to taste

Place the onion, garlic, ham hock, corn, celery, carrot, rosemary, thyme, and broth in a large stockpot and bring to a boil over high heat. Reduce the heat to low and cook until the ham hock is tender, about 1 hour.

Remove the ham hock and corncobs from the broth and when they are cool enough to handle, remove the meat from the ham hock and the kernels from the cobs. Chop the meat and return the meat and the corn kernels to the broth. Set aside.

Place a large straight-sided nonreactive saucepan over medium-high heat and when it is hot, add the oil. Add the rice and toast it, about 2 minutes. Add the wine and cook, stirring, until it has been absorbed by the rice, about 2 minutes.

Add 1 cup of the broth and cook, stirring constantly, until it has been absorbed by the rice. Continue adding the broth, 1 cup at a time, stirring well after each addition, until all the liquid has been absorbed by the rice, about 18 to 20 minutes.

Add the butter, if desired, and the red beans, salt, and pepper, and stir until the beans are heated through, about 2 minutes. Serve immediately, garnished with the cilantro, scallions, and Parmesan cheese.

GARLIC-LOBSTER RISOTTO CALABRESE

*W*hen I was fifteen, we moved from Atlanta to Connecticut. Afterward, we and a few other families made an annual trip to a little town in coastal Maine called Camden (where the original *Peyton Place* was filmed). Every morning after breakfast, we took a long walk around the harbor, eventually ending up at the lobster pound to pick up about twenty-five or thirty chicken lobsters, and then on to a local farm stand to buy fresh corn, lettuce, and freshly dug potatoes, with which my mother made fresh potato chips. To cook the lobster and corn, she built a stacked-box-steamer contraption that sat on the beach on top of a fire with a trough of ocean water around it. The seawater would boil and create steam that wove its way through the stacked wire-mesh boxes and cooked things as they were stacked, according to size. We feasted long into the night. No lobster ever compares to the ones I ate in Camden, so I rarely eat it whole.

You must be a garlic lover to like this dish, or have a really bad cold. It is infused with an intense garlic flavor at every step. The creamy arborio rice is a perfect medium for the richness of the garlic and the lobster. You may substitute shrimp for the lobster.

Serve this with Swordfish with Clams (page 308) and a green salad with Shallot Vinaigrette (page 33), or as the centerpiece of a summer meal.

SERVES 4 TO 6 AS AN ENTRÉE OR 8 TO 10 AS A SIDE DISH

LOBSTER CREAM:
1 tablespoon olive oil
2 to 3 garlic cloves, thinly sliced
2 fresh or canned plum tomatoes, diced
Grated zest of 1 lemon

2 tablespoons chopped fresh oregano leaves

¾ cup light cream

1 pound cooked lobster meat, chopped (about 3 cups), or the meat from
three 1-pound lobsters

GARLIC RISOTTO:

1 tablespoon olive oil

1 cup diced slab bacon or diced high-quality thick-sliced lean bacon

1 red or Spanish onion, finely diced

3 to 4 garlic cloves, minced

2 cups chopped fresh or canned tomatoes, drained and diced

½ to 1 teaspoon crushed red pepper flakes

2 cups arborio rice

1 cup dry white wine

5 cups Lobster Stock (page 42), Chicken Broth (page 38), or water

1 teaspoon kosher salt

½ teaspoon black pepper

2 tablespoons chopped fresh flat-leaf parsley leaves, for garnish

To make the lobster cream: Place a medium skillet over medium-high heat and when it is hot, add the oil. Add the garlic and tomatoes and cook until the garlic is golden and the tomatoes have the consistency of a sauce, about 5 minutes. Add the lemon zest, oregano, and cream and cook for 3 minutes. Take the pan off the heat and add the lobster. Set aside and keep warm.

To make the garlic risotto: Place a large straight-sided saucepan over medium heat and when it is hot, add the olive oil and bacon. When the bacon begins to render its fat, add the onion and garlic. Cook until the onion is soft, about 5 minutes.

Add the tomatoes and red pepper flakes and cook, stirring occasionally, for 10 minutes or until the tomatoes have the consistency of a sauce. Add the rice and stir until it is well coated.

Add the wine and 1 cup of the water or stock and cook, stirring constantly, until the liquid has been absorbed by the rice. Continue adding the liquid, 1 cup at a time, stirring well after each addition, until it has all been absorbed by the rice, about 18 to 20 minutes. Add the salt and pepper.

To serve, ladle the risotto into shallow bowls and top with the lobster cream. Garnish with the parsley.

GREEN APPLE RISOTTO WITH CABBAGE AND BACON

*A*pples, cabbage, and bacon is a classic combination. In order to create a contrast with the creamy rice, you must use a really tart crisp apple. This is an interesting accompaniment to duck, chicken, or pork.

SERVES 4 AS A SIDE DISH

½ cup chopped slab bacon or chopped high-quality thick-sliced lean bacon
2 garlic cloves, chopped
½ Savoy cabbage, thinly sliced
1 teaspoon kosher salt
1 teaspoon black pepper
1½ cups arborio rice
3½ cups water
1½ cups apple cider
1 Granny Smith apple, peeled, cored, and cut into small dice
1 tablespoon Dijon mustard
⅓ cup chopped scallions
2 tablespoons unsalted butter, at room temperature (optional)

Place a large straight-sided nonreactive saucepan over medium heat and when it is hot, add the bacon. When the bacon has rendered its fat, add the garlic, cabbage, salt, and pepper, stirring well after each addition, and cook until the cabbage is wilted and tender, about 10 minutes. Add the rice and stir until it is well coated.

Add 1 cup of water and cook, stirring constantly, until the liquid has been absorbed by the rice. Add ½ cup apple cider and continue adding water and apple cider, 1 cup at a time, stirring well after each addition, until all the liquid has been absorbed, about 18 to 20 minutes.

Stir in the apple, mustard, scallions, and, if desired, the butter. Serve immediately.

CREAMY CHESTNUT RISOTTO

*I*ntense and sweet, chestnuts work well with creamy risotto. We also use this creamy chestnut puree to fill ravioli. This unusual combination complements venison, Simple Roasted Chicken (page 244), or grilled swordfish.

SERVES 4 TO 6 AS A SIDE DISH

1½ cups peeled fresh, canned, or frozen chestnuts, about 1 pound
    (see next page)
1 Spanish onion, minced
½ cup heavy cream
8½ cups Chicken Broth (page 38) or canned low-sodium chicken broth
¼ cup maple syrup
1 teaspoon fresh thyme leaves
2 cups arborio rice
1 cup dry white wine
2 tablespoons unsalted butter, at room temperature (optional)
1 teaspoon salt
½ teaspoon pepper

CHESTNUT GARNISH:
1 tablespoon unsalted butter
½ cup fresh, canned, or frozen chestnuts (about ⅓ pound), thinly sliced
    (see next page)
¼ cup grated Parmesan cheese
¼ cup finely chopped scallions
1 orange, peeled and separated into segments
2 tablespoons chopped fresh flat-leaf parsley

Place the chestnuts, the onion, the cream, ½ cup of the chicken broth, the maple syrup, and the thyme in a medium-size saucepan and bring to a boil over high heat. Reduce the heat to medium and cook until the chestnuts are very tender, about 15 to 20 minutes. Transfer to a blender and puree. Set aside.

To make the garnish: Melt the butter in a small skillet over medium-high heat. Add the sliced chestnuts and cook until browned, about 4 minutes. Set aside.

Place a large straight-sided saucepan over medium-high heat and when it is hot, add the rice. When the rice is hot, add the wine and cook, stirring, until it has been absorbed by the rice, about 2 minutes.

Add 1 cup broth and cook, stirring constantly, until it has been absorbed by the rice. Continue adding broth 1 cup at a time, stirring well after each addition, until all the liquid has been absorbed by the rice, about 18 to 20 minutes. Add the chestnut puree, the butter, if desired, and the salt and pepper.

Garnish the risotto with the browned chestnuts, Parmesan, scallions, orange segments, and parsley. Serve immediately.

■ *Chestnuts can be purchased fresh in the fall and early winter. To roast fresh chestnuts, slash "X" on the flat side of each one. Preheat the oven to 425 degrees. Place the chestnuts on a baking sheet in the oven and roast until they are soft when pierced with a knife, about 20 minutes. When they have cooled slightly but are still hot, peel them.*

PASTA AND BEANS .

TORTELLI OF BUTTERNUT SQUASH WITH BROWN BUTTER

*S*weet, nutty, and delicate, this is one of my favorite dishes, and it has never left the menu at Olives.

SERVES 8 AS AN APPETIZER OR 6 AS AN ENTRÉE;
MAKES 40 TO 42 TORTELLI

BUTTERNUT SQUASH FILLING:
2 tablespoons unsalted butter
5 to 6 cups diced peeled butternut squash (about 1 large or 2 small)
½ cup ground amaretti cookies
½ cup fresh bread crumbs
¼ cup finely grated Parmesan cheese
¼ teaspoon ground nutmeg
1½ teaspoons kosher salt
¼ teaspoon black pepper

DOUGH:
2 to 2½ cups all-purpose flour
1 teaspoon kosher salt
2 large eggs
3 large egg yolks
Semolina for sprinkling

BROWN BUTTER:
1 cup (2 sticks) unsalted butter
1 tablespoon chopped fresh sage leaves
1 teaspoon kosher salt
½ teaspoon black pepper

Grated Parmesan cheese for serving

To make the filling: Melt the butter in a large skillet over medium-heat and add the butternut squash. Cook until the squash is just starting to caramelize and is golden brown, about 10 minutes. Add water to cover and cook until the squash is tender, about 20 minutes. Drain.

Transfer the squash to a food processor fitted with a metal blade. Add the amaretti, bread crumbs, Parmesan cheese, nutmeg, salt, and pepper and blend until smooth.

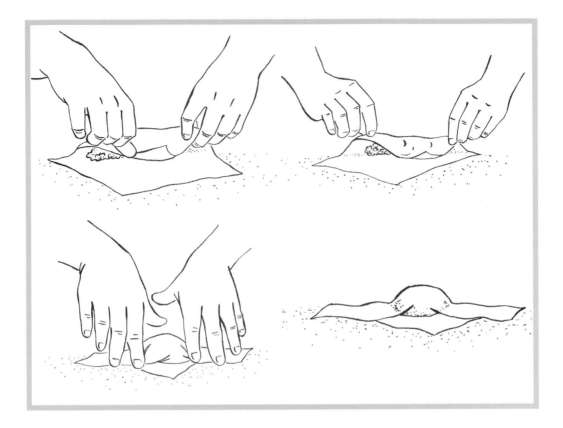

To make the dough: Flour a large cutting board or work surface. Place 2 cups of the flour and the salt on the board and make a wide well in it. Place the eggs and egg yolks in the well. With a fork, follow the perimeter of the well, bringing in small amounts of flour and continuing all the way around, until gradually most of the flour is absorbed. If necessary, add up to ½ cup of the remaining flour.

Divide the dough into 2 pieces. Put the dough through a pasta machine, folding into halves each time and then reinserting 15 to 20 times, to knead it. Continue until the pasta is paper-thin. Lay out the sheets of dough and cut them into 4-inch squares; you should have about 40 to 42 squares.

Place 1 heaping tablespoon of the filling on one corner of each square. Fold over the filled portion, press down around the filling, and place on a baking sheet lined with wax paper and sprinkled with semolina.

To make the brown butter: Melt the butter in a large skillet over medium-high heat and cook until it begins to foam and brown, about 4 minutes. Add the sage, salt, and pepper

Bring a large pot of water—salted, if desired—to a boil over high heat. Add the tortelli and cook until they are tender, about 3 minutes. Toss with the brown butter and Parmesan and serve immediately.

■ *FRESH PASTA*

After years of teaching cooking classes, I've finally realized that almost no one makes fresh pasta at home, a sad fact for someone who feels almost fanatical about it.

My pasta training in Italy (basically following around older Italian women in their kitchens as they made pasta) taught me many things: fresh pasta is essentially eggs and flour, sometimes with the addition of wine, water, vegetables, or extra egg yolks for enrichment. Pasta should be made by hand: Make a well of flour (as you would for gravy, in mashed potatoes) and drop the eggs in that well. With a fork, follow the perimeter of the well, bringing in small amounts of flour and continuing all the way around, until gradually most of the flour is absorbed. Once the dough is formed, with the palm of your hand, start kneading the dough, and knead until there is no flour left.

Pasta, especially ravioli, should be tender and silken in texture. You should never have to struggle with fork and knife. When you put a ravioli in your mouth, it should explode with flavor and pouf!! The dough should be light, tender, delicate, and ethereal; the filling, remarkable. The worst criticism of a ravioli is the question "What was in that?"

LENTIL AND GRAIN CHILI WITH CUCUMBER RAITA

*L*entils are one of my favorite legumes. Unfortunately, they are underrated and most of us don't eat them often enough. Rich in flavor and low in fat, they are meaty and filling and make a hearty and heartwarming meal. Although the chili can be served without the raita, a classic Indian condiment, the combination of the hot and cold, cool and spicy makes for a dish with intriguing contrasts.

This is the perfect meal for a Super Bowl party or a cold rainy Sunday, and a great alternative to meat chili. The raita can also be served on chilled poached salmon or a leg of lamb sandwich.

SERVES 6 TO 8

1 tablespoon olive oil
2 tablespoons chopped peeled fresh ginger
6 garlic cloves, chopped
1 large Spanish onion, chopped
3 medium carrots, peeled and chopped
2 celery stalks, chopped
1 small jalapeño or Scotch bonnet pepper, seeded and minced
2 chipotle (smoked jalapeño) peppers, seeded and minced
1 20-ounce can crushed tomatoes
2 to 3 tablespoons chili powder
1 tablespoon ground cumin
1 teaspoon chopped fresh oregano leaves or ⅓ teaspoon dried oregano
2 cups brown lentils, rinsed and picked over
1 cup cooked chick peas, rinsed
½ cup barley
½ cup bulgur wheat

8 to 10 cups Chicken Broth (page 38) or canned low-sodium chicken broth
1 teaspoon kosher salt
½ teaspoon black pepper
Cucumber Raita (recipe follows)

Place a large stockpot over medium heat and when it is hot, add the olive oil. Add the ginger, garlic, onion, carrots, and celery, stirring well after each addition, and cook until the vegetables are soft, about 10 minutes.

Add the jalapeño pepper, chipotle peppers, tomatoes, chili powder, cumin, oregano, lentils, chick peas, barley, bulgur wheat, stock, salt, and pepper, stirring well after each addition, increase the heat to high, and bring to a boil. Reduce the heat to low and cook until the lentils are soft, about 1 hour.

Top each serving with a dollop of cucumber raita.

CUCUMBER RAITA

2 cups plain lowfat yogurt
1 red onion, quartered and thinly sliced
1 English cucumber, peeled, seeded, and grated
¼ cup fresh lemon juice (about 1 lemon)
1 tablespoon chopped fresh mint leaves
1 tablespoon chopped fresh cilantro leaves

Line a colander with cheesecloth or muslin. Place a large bowl under the colander. Place the yogurt in the colander and let sit at room temperature for about 4 hours or cover and refrigerate overnight.

Place the drained yogurt in a medium-sized bowl. Discard the liquid that has drained into the bowl. Add the onion, cucumber, lemon juice, mint, and cilantro and mix well. Cover and refrigerate until ready to serve, up to 6 hours.

CHILLED BLACK OLIVE SPAGHETTI SALAD

As a rule, I dislike cold pasta salads, but for this one I make an exception. Serve this by itself or place it in a large serving bowl, make a well in the center, and fill it with tomato and mozzarella salad.

SERVES 4 TO 6

1 pound spaghetti
2 tablespoons olive oil
4 garlic cloves, thinly sliced
4 anchovy fillets, minced
2 tablespoons capers, chopped
2 cups cured black olives, such as Kalamata, Gaeta, or oil-cured, pitted
½ teaspoon kosher salt
¼ to ½ teaspoon black pepper
2 tablespoons balsamic vinegar
1 tablespoon chopped fresh rosemary leaves
Shaved Parmesan cheese, for garnish

Bring a large pot of water to a boil over high heat and add the spaghetti. Cook until tender, drain, and rinse under cold water. Set aside.

Place a medium-size skillet over medium-high heat and when it is hot, add 1 tablespoon of the oil. Add the garlic, anchovy fillets, capers, and olives and cook until they are lightly toasted, about 5 to 7 minutes. Transfer the olive mixture to a food processor. While the machine is running, gradually add the remaining 1 tablespoon oil, the salt, pepper, and vinegar. Process until the mixture is completely smooth.

Add the olive paste and rosemary to the spaghetti, toss well, and serve immediately, with shaved Parmesan cheese.

COUNTRY SHELLS WITH SAUSAGE, CANNELLINI BEANS, AND SPINACH

*T*his is a hearty dish that's perfect for a fall or winter day. It's a complete meal in itself and very quick to prepare. Serve it with a loaf of bread and a glass of Zinfandel.

SERVES 4 TO 6

1 tablespoon olive oil
1 carrot, peeled and diced
1 celery stalk, diced
1 Spanish onion, diced
1 pound spicy Italian sausage, removed from casings
½ cup dry red wine
1 16-ounce can plum tomatoes, including juice, chopped
2 tablespoons tomato paste
1 pound medium pasta shells, rigatoni, or ziti
1 cup cooked white cannellini beans, rinsed
1 bunch leaf spinach, well washed, stems removed, and leaves roughly
    chopped (about 10 ounces)
½ bunch fresh flat-leaf parsley, leaves only, chopped
¼ cup grated Parmesan cheese
1 teaspoon kosher salt
½ teaspoon black pepper
2 tablespoons light or heavy cream (optional)

Place a large skillet over medium-high heat and when it is hot, add the oil. Add the carrot, celery, and onion and cook until the vegetables are soft, about 7 minutes. Add the sausage and cook, crumbling it with a fork, until it has rendered its fat and is no longer pink. Discard the fat and reduce the heat to medium-low. Add the red wine, tomatoes with their juice, and tomato paste and simmer until the sauce has thickened, about 20 minutes.

Meanwhile, bring a large pot of water to a boil over high heat. Add the pasta shells and cook until tender. Drain well.

Add the beans, spinach, parsley, Parmesan cheese, salt, pepper, and, if desired, the cream to the tomato sauce. Cook until the spinach is wilted and the beans are heated through.

Toss the cooked pasta with the sauce and serve immediately.

Eggplant and Red Lentils with Pasta

*T*here was a time in my life when I wanted to stop eating meat but I wasn't quite ready to give up the heartiness and texture. This recipe satisfied both needs. To make this into a great soup, add more chicken broth and eliminate the pasta.

You can prepare this sauce ahead and reheat it just before serving.

SERVES 6 TO 8

¼ cup olive oil
3 garlic cloves, thinly sliced
2 medium-size eggplants, peeled and cubed
2 teaspoons kosher salt
1 teaspoon black pepper
1 Spanish onion, diced
1½ cups red lentils, rinsed and picked over
1 tablespoon curry powder
2 teaspoons ground cumin
2 bay leaves
2 cups canned crushed tomatoes
6 to 10 cups Chicken Broth (page 38) or canned low-sodium chicken broth
1 pound orecchiette pasta
¼ cup fresh cilantro leaves, roughly chopped, for garnish
¼ cup fresh basil leaves, roughly chopped, for garnish
¼ cup fresh roughly chopped scallion greens, for garnish
Shaved Pecorino cheese, for garnish

Place a large skillet over medium-high heat and when it is hot, add the oil. Add the garlic and cook until it is lightly browned, about 2 to 3 minutes.

Add the eggplant, salt, and pepper and cook the eggplant, in batches if necessary, until it is soft and lightly browned, about 5 minutes.

Add the onion and cook for 3 minutes. Add the lentils, curry, cumin, and bay leaves, stirring well after each addition, and cook for 5 minutes.

Reduce the heat to medium and add 6 cups of chicken broth. Cook until the lentils are soft, about 45 minutes, adding more broth as necessary. Add the tomatoes and cook until the sauce is thickened, about 15 to 20 minutes.

While the sauce is cooking, bring a large pot of water to a boil over high heat. Add the pasta and cook until it is tender. Drain.

Remove the bay leaf from the lentil mixture and toss the mixture with the pasta. Garnish with the cilantro, basil, scallion greens, and Pecorino. Serve immediately.

PASTA E FAGIOLI WITH PAPPARDELLE AND SHRIMP

*P*asta e Fagioli is one of the most intelligent combinations ever created, not only because of its nutritional content but because it is one of the most extraordinary combinations of flavors: smoky, sweet, creamy, and salty. You'd think I could just leave it alone, but I can't—the traditional small pasta is replaced by very wide pappardelle noodles, while the addition of shrimp adds a snap of flavor and a meaty texture.

SERVES 4 TO 6

1 tablespoon olive oil, plus ½ cup additional (optional)
1 cup chopped slab bacon or chopped high-quality thick-sliced lean bacon or
   1 ham hock
1 small Spanish onion, chopped
5 garlic cloves, finely chopped
2 carrots, peeled and chopped
1 celery stalk, chopped
1½ tablespoons chopped fresh rosemary leaves
3 cups cooked navy or pinto beans, rinsed
2 to 3 cups Chicken Broth (page 38) or canned low-sodium chicken broth
¾ pound pappardelle, spaghetti, or fettuccine

SHRIMP:
1 tablespoon olive oil
1¼ pounds large shrimp (about 20), peeled and deveined
½ teaspoon kosher salt
½ teaspoon black pepper
2 garlic cloves, thinly sliced
½ cup dry white wine

¼ cup chopped fresh flat-leaf parsley leaves
2 tablespoons chopped scallion greens
¼ to ½ cup grated Parmesan cheese
¼ to ½ teaspoon crushed red pepper flakes
1 tablespoon unsalted butter, at room temperature (optional)
Fresh rosemary sprigs, for garnish

Place a large saucepan over low heat and add the 1 tablespoon oil. Add the bacon and cook until it begins to render its fat, about 2 minutes. Add the onion, garlic, carrots, celery, and rosemary, stirring well after each addition, and cook until the onion is soft, about 4 to 5 minutes. Increase the heat to medium and add the beans and 2 cups of the chicken broth. Simmer, adding more broth if necessary, until the liquid has been absorbed and the beans begin to break apart, about 30 minutes.

Transfer the bean mixture to a blender or a food processor fitted with a steel blade and puree, gradually adding up to ½ cup olive oil, if desired, for a creamier, richer puree. Set aside.

Bring a large pot of water to a boil over high heat. Add the pasta and cook until tender. Drain the pasta, reserving 1 cup of the pasta water.

Meanwhile, cook the shrimp: Place a large skillet over medium heat and when it is hot, add the oil. Sprinkle the shrimp with the salt and pepper. Add the shrimp to the skillet and cook until it is pink and opaque throughout, about 3 minutes. Add the wine and cook until somewhat reduced, about 2 minutes. Stir in the bean puree and, if the puree seems too thick, add some of the reserved pasta water. Add the pasta and cook until just heated through. Add the parsley, scallion greens, cheese, red pepper flakes, and, if desired, the butter, stirring well after each addition.

Serve in broad flat bowls, garnished with fresh rosemary sprigs.

SPAGHETTI WITH TRUFFLE MASCARPONE

*I*nspired by a great dish, Spaghetti Lucullus, named after the Roman general and gastronome, Spaghetti with Truffle Mascarpone is meant to be served, spun around a fork, with a small dollop of osetra caviar. Like the Black Truffle, Potato, and Parsnip "Risotto" (page 164), it is as easy to make as it is expensive.

Try it as a starter for a special meal or whenever you have an extra truffle or two sitting around (I'm only kidding). It's the perfect dish for New Year's Eve, accompanied by a good champagne.

SERVES 6 TO 8 AS AN APPETIZER

1 pound spaghetti
4 tablespoons unsalted butter
6 to 8 shallots, thinly sliced
1 cup heavy cream
½ cup dry white wine
½ cup Chicken Broth (page 38) or canned low-sodium chicken broth
¼ cup canned truffle peelings
1 to 2 tablespoons truffle oil
2 tablespoons mascarpone
1 teaspoon kosher salt
1 teaspoon black pepper
2 tablespoons grated Parmesan cheese, plus more for garnish
2 tablespoons chopped fresh flat-leaf parsley leaves, for garnish

Bring a large pot of water to a boil over high heat. Add the spaghetti and cook until tender. Drain the spaghetti, reserving 1 cup of the pasta water.

Melt the butter in a large skillet over medium heat. Add the shallots and cook until they are lightly browned, about 7 to 9 minutes. Add the cream, wine, and chicken broth and simmer for 2 minutes. Add the truffle peelings, spaghetti, and, if desired, ½ to 1 cup of the pasta water and cook for 1 minute.

Toss with the truffle oil, mascarpone, salt, pepper, and Parmesan cheese. Garnish with Parmesan and parsley and serve immediately.

LOBSTER BOLOGNESE

*B*olognese sauce, which varies from household to household in Italy, is a meat sauce that originated in Bologna. Traditionally it is made with pork, veal, or beef or a combination of all three; it also contains pancetta, carrots, onions, celery, tomatoes, rosemary, oregano, basil, and flat-leaf parsley. The ingredients are stewed together and finished with cream, butter, and Parmesan cheese. I, among others, am guilty of replacing the usual meats with just about anything else. Using seafood means a shorter cooking time; otherwise, this recipe follows the classic recipe fairly closely.

Lobster Bolognese has been on the menu at Olives for a long, long time. I came up with it as an economical way to serve lobster in the winter, when the prices skyrocket beyond their usual exorbitant price. It can also be made with diced salmon or shrimp.

SERVES 4 AS AN ENTRÉE

2 tablespoons olive oil
½ Spanish onion, cut into small dice
1 carrot, peeled and cut into small dice
1 celery stalk, cut into small dice
1 cup dry white wine
6 cups Lobster Stock (page 42)
1 cup chopped fresh or canned tomatoes
½ cup light or heavy cream
1 tablespoon unsalted butter
½ pound cooked fresh lobster meat, chopped (about 2 cups)
¾ pound pappardelle

Place a large skillet over medium-high heat and when it is hot, add the oil. Add the onion, carrot, and celery and cook for 5 minutes. Add the wine and cook for 5 minutes. Add the lobster stock and tomatoes and cook until the liquid has reduced by two thirds, about 20 minutes.

Add the cream and butter and cook for 3 minutes. Add the lobster meat.

While the sauce is cooking, bring a large pot of water to a boil over high heat. Add the pappardelle and cook until tender. Drain. Add the pasta to the lobster sauce and serve immediately.

Free-Form Tuscan-Style Rabbit Lasagna

*T*o make this dish, you must first forget all your preconceived notions about lasagna. Yes, it's a layered pasta dish, but it doesn't have to be layered in any particular manner. Then you must forget all your warm and fuzzy feelings about rabbits. When I was growing up (and even today), my all-time favorite cartoon character was Bugs Bunny. Even so, rabbit is my favorite meal, and if you try it, you'll agree it's delicate, refined, and flavorful.

This is a time-consuming dish but not a difficult one to prepare. When you have less time, you can serve the ragù on polenta or pasta. If you can't deal with rabbit, it's fine to substitute chicken. If you don't want to use fresh pasta, try an equal weight of no-boil pasta sheets.

Serve this with Garlic-Roasted Radicchio (page 137).

SERVES 8

RABBIT RAGÙ:
⅓ cup olive oil
2 3-pound rabbits, cut into serving pieces
2 teaspoons kosher salt
2 teaspoons black pepper
1 large Spanish onion, finely minced
2 to 3 carrots, peeled and finely minced
3 celery stalks, finely minced
6 garlic cloves, finely minced
2 tablespoons fresh rosemary leaves, finely minced
2 bay leaves
2 medium-size portobello mushrooms, trimmed, wiped clean, and cut into
*   medium dice (or 2 cups diced white button mushrooms)*
2 cups chopped fresh or canned tomatoes
1½ cups dry red wine

1½ cups dry white wine

1 cup balsamic vinegar

5 cups Chicken Broth (page 38), Dark Stock (page 40), canned low-sodium chicken broth, or water

1 cup heavy or light cream

2 tablespoons unsalted butter (optional)

½ to ¾ pound fresh lasagna sheets (approximately 12 to 16 sheets, 7 by 7 inches)

½ cup part-skim ricotta cheese

½ cup shredded Fontina cheese

2 tablespoons grated Parmesan cheese

1 tablespoon chopped fresh flat-leaf parsley leaves

To make the rabbit ragù: Place a 14-inch skillet over medium-high heat and when it is hot, add the oil. Sprinkle the rabbit with the salt and pepper and add it to the pan, one piece at a time, being sure that the pan is hot prior to each addition. Cook until the rabbit is lightly browned, about 10 to 12 minutes per side. Cook the rabbit in batches if necessary. Remove the rabbit from the pan and set it aside.

Reheat the pan and add the onion, carrots, celery, and garlic, stirring well after each addition, and cook for 2 minutes. Add the rosemary, bay leaves, and mushrooms. Add the chopped tomatoes, red and white wines, balsamic vinegar, and broth and the reserved rabbit pieces. Bring to a simmer, reduce the heat to low, and cook for 2 minutes. Continue cooking, uncovered, until the liquid has reduced by one half, about 1 hour.

Remove the rabbit (letting the ragù continue to simmer) and when it is cool enough to handle, remove the meat and discard the skin and bones. Set the meat aside.

Continue cooking the ragù for an additional 10 minutes. Off the heat, add the cream, butter, and reserved rabbit meat to the pan.

Bring a large pot of water to a boil over high heat. Add the lasagna sheets and cook until they are al dente. Drain and add them, one at a time, to the ragù. There should be a little more sauce than lasagna sheets.

Combine the ricotta, Fontina, and Parmesan cheeses in a bowl.

To assemble the lasagna: Place about 2 cups of ragù in a large skillet and dot it with about ⅓ cup of the cheese mixture. Repeat two times, ending with cheese on top. Sprinkle with the parsley.

Place the pan over low heat and cook until the cheese has completely melted, about 10 minutes. (If you prefer a baked lasagna, assemble the lasagna in a greased 8 x 12-inch pan and bake it in a preheated 350-degree oven for 10 minutes.)

Let rest for 10 minutes before serving.

PENNE WITH LOBSTER AND GREEN TOMATO SAUCE

*L*ike most New Englanders, I'm always trying to figure out what to do with the extra green tomatoes from my garden. After many attempts to fry them creatively, I came up with this sauce, which perfectly pairs the tangy green tomato with rich lobster. The problem was that it became a big hit at Olives, and I couldn't get green tomatoes all year long. My solution was to substitute an equal amount of tomatillos.

Try this sauce with braised shellfish, clams, shrimp, tuna, or swordfish or steamed halibut.

SERVES 4 AS AN ENTRÉE OR 6 TO 8 AS AN APPETIZER

2 1½- to 2-pound lobsters
2 tablespoons olive oil
1 Spanish onion, chopped
4 garlic cloves, thinly sliced
5 to 6 green tomatoes or 12 to 15 tomatillos, peeled and chopped
1 tablespoon chopped fresh oregano leaves, plus 2 whole sprigs for garnish
4 cups Chicken Broth (page 38) or canned low-sodium chicken broth
1 pound penne
3 ounces thinly sliced prosciutto, julienned
⅔ cup grated Parmesan cheese, plus additional for serving
¼ teaspoon kosher salt
½ teaspoon black pepper

Bring a large pot of water to a boil over high heat. Add the lobsters and boil for 6 to 8 minutes. Drain (reserve the liquid for Lobster Stock, page 42). When the lobsters are cool enough to handle, remove the tail meat and roughly chop it. Reserve the claws for garnish.

To make the green tomato sauce: Place a saucepan over medium heat and when it is hot, add 1 tablespoon of the oil. Add the onion and 2 of the garlic cloves and cook for 2 minutes. Add the green tomatoes and oregano and cook until the tomatoes are very soft, about 7 to 10 minutes. Add the chicken broth and cook until reduced by one-third, about 15 minutes. Transfer the mixture to a blender or a food processor fitted with a steel blade and puree. Set the sauce and the saucepan aside.

Bring a large pot of water to a boil over high heat. Add the penne and cook until tender. Drain well.

In the meantime, reheat the skillet over medium-high heat and add the remaining 1 tablespoon oil. Add the remaining 2 garlic cloves and cook for 1 to 2 minutes. Add the lobster tail meat, prosciutto, Parmesan, salt, and pepper, stirring well after each addition, and cook for 2 minutes, stirring constantly. Add the green tomato sauce and cook until it is hot, about 3 minutes.

Toss the penne with the sauce, stirring well. Transfer the mixture to a serving platter and garnish with the lobster claws, oregano sprigs, and additional Parmesan cheese.

POULTRY ▪

TAHINI-MARINATED CHICKEN WITH HONEY, YOGURT, AND GINGER SAUCE

*T*his dish is simply luscious. The nutty flavor of the tahini combines beautifully with the sweet honey and tart yogurt. Serve hot or chilled, with basmati rice and sautéed broccoli rabe or Broccoli Rabe with Sausage (page 143).

SERVES 4

TAHINI MARINADE:
3 scallions (white part only), chopped
1 tablespoon minced peeled fresh ginger
2 garlic cloves
2 tablespoons sesame tahini
½ cup plain yogurt
½ cup water

4 whole boneless, skinless chicken breasts
1 tablespoon olive oil
1 teaspoon kosher salt
½ teaspoon black pepper

HONEY, YOGURT, AND GINGER SAUCE:
2 teaspoons olive oil
1 tablespoon minced peeled fresh ginger
¼ cup chopped scallions
⅓ cup honey
½ cup plain yogurt

To make the tahini marinade: Place the scallions, ginger, garlic, tahini, yogurt, and water in a food processor fitted with a steel blade and blend until it has a creamy consistency. Place it in a large bowl and add the chicken breasts. Cover and refrigerate for at least 4 hours, or overnight.

Place a large pan over medium-high heat and when it is hot, add the oil. Remove the chicken breasts from the marinade, discarding the marinade. Sprinkle the chicken breasts with salt and pepper and add them to the pan. Cook until they are golden, about 4 to 5 minutes per side. Set aside.

To make the sauce: Place a medium pan over medium-high heat and when it is hot, add the oil. Add the ginger, scallions, and honey and cook for 1 to 2 minutes. Let cool slightly, then add the yogurt. Serve over the chicken.

SPICY LOW-FAT CHICKEN PATTY

*I*n my everlasting struggle to eat healthfully and stay fit, I came up with this as a spicy substitute for the fat-laden hamburger. I like to add the egg whites for the additional protein and the oats for the creaminess but you can eliminate both and substitute 1½ pounds ground chicken for the chopped chicken breast. Serve with baked potatoes or spicy oven-roasted potatoes.

■ *Three ounces of boneless, skinless chicken breast has 24 grams of protein, 1.5 grams of fat, and 116 calories.*

SERVES 4 TO 6

1¼ pounds boneless, skinless chicken breasts, trimmed of fat and finely
    chopped by hand
½ bunch scallions, finely chopped
½ cup finely chopped fresh cilantro leaves
1½ tablespoons finely chopped peeled fresh ginger
2 garlic cloves, finely chopped
1 teaspoon grainy mustard
½ to 1 teaspoon Vietnamese chili paste
3 large egg whites or 2 large eggs
1¼ cups quick-cooking oats, coarsely ground in a blender or food processor
1 teaspoon kosher salt
½ teaspoon black pepper
Juice of 1 lemon or lime

Preheat the oven to 350 degrees.

Place all the ingredients except the lemon juice in a medium-size mixing bowl and mix well. Shape into 6 patties.

Place a large ovenproof nonstick skillet over medium heat and when it is hot, add the patties. Cook until deeply browned, about 4 minutes on each side.

Transfer the skillet to the oven and bake for about 8 minutes, or until the patties are thoroughly cooked. Drizzle with the lemon juice and serve immediately.

OLIVE-CRUSTED CHICKEN WITH PUREE OF FENNEL AND TOMATO

*C*hicken is a great canvas for the rustic flavors of this Provençal-inspired dish. Sweet, salty, and sour, this is not your typical come-home-and-whip-up-dinner chicken. But once you assemble the different elements, it's a snap. Both the puree and the crust can be made ahead of time. Serve with Everyday Polenta (page 180).

SERVES 4

PUREE OF FENNEL AND TOMATO:
⅓ cup chopped slab bacon or chopped high-quality thick-sliced lean bacon
3 garlic cloves, thinly sliced
1 fennel bulb, trimmed, cored, and thinly sliced
1 cup chopped fresh or canned tomatoes
1 cup dry white wine
3½ cups Chicken Broth (page 38) or canned low-sodium chicken broth
¼ teaspoon crushed red pepper flakes

OLIVE CRUST:
4 Ligurian olives or other black olives, pitted and coarsely chopped
Grated zest and juice of ½ lemon
½ cup golden raisins, chopped
1½ teaspoons capers
1½ cups coarse toasted bread cubes (½-inch cubes)
2 tablespoons finely grated Parmesan cheese
1 small egg
1½ tablespoons chopped fresh flat-leaf parsley leaves

*1 tablespoon Black Olive Paste (page 46) or store-bought
    (San Remo brand is good)*
1 tablespoon olive oil

2 whole skinless, boneless chicken breasts, halved
1 teaspoon kosher salt
1 teaspoon black pepper

Preheat the oven to 425 degrees.

To make the puree: Place a large skillet over medium heat and when it is hot, add the bacon. When it begins to render its fat, add the garlic and cook for about 5 minutes, stirring occasionally. Add the fennel, tomatoes, wine, chicken broth, and red pepper flakes, stirring well after each addition, and cook until the vegetables are soft, about 25 minutes. Transfer the contents to a food processor fitted with a steel blade or a blender and puree. Set aside.

To make the crust: Place the olives, lemon zest and juice, raisins, and capers, ¼ cup of the bread cubes, and the Parmesan cheese in a food processor fitted with a steel blade and pulse until coarsely chopped. Add the egg, parsley, olive paste, and oil and pulse to mix. Set aside.

Reheat the skillet and add the oil. Sprinkle the chicken with the salt and pepper, add it to the pan, one piece at a time, skinned side down, and cook until the chicken is deeply browned on the skinned side only, about 3 to 4 minutes. Transfer to a plate.

Divide the olive mixture into 4 portions and place it on the browned side of the chicken, patting it down to form a crust. Top with the remaining 1¼ cups bread crumbs.

Place the puree in a large skillet over medium heat and when the puree just begins to bubble, add the chicken, crust side up. Cook until the chicken is tender, about 20 to 25 minutes.

Preheat the broiler. Place the skillet under the broiler and broil for about 3 minutes, or until the crust is crisp and browned.

Divide the puree among four plates and top with the olive-crusted chicken breasts.

ROAST CHICKEN WITH HERB AND LEMON PASTE

A simple roast chicken is one of the great pleasures in life and the test of a good kitchen. Perfectly roasted chicken has crisp skin and tender meat. At Olives we spit-roast our chickens over a live fire, which adds char to the skin and smokiness to the meat. The spinning motion of the rotisserie allows the bird to self-baste. If you have a chance, try this method.

I believe in hormone-free chickens, but the quality of the chicken is the more important factor in taste. This has more to do with the strain of bird than how it is raised. My favorite variety is any type that derives from the Bresse chicken, from France (you can't get them here—only in Europe). Don't use frozen chicken (freezing dries the meat out), free-range birds (you can't be sure they're really free-range), or yellow-skinned ones (sorry, Frank). Try to stay with hormone-free chickens.

Serve with Garlic Mashed Potatoes (page 175).

■ *When cooking chicken at this temperature, it is critical that you have a clean oven and good ventilation. If you don't have either, skip this recipe or set the oven at 350 degrees and increase the roasting time to 50 to 60 minutes.*

It may seem like a lot of extra work to sear the chicken on the stove, but the crispy skin and moist meat are well worth it.

SERVES 4

HERB AND LEMON PASTE:
1 Spanish onion, coarsely chopped
1 cup chopped fresh basil leaves

½ cup chopped fresh flat-leaf parsley leaves
2 tablespoons chopped fresh rosemary leaves
2 tablespoons chopped fresh mint leaves
1 tablespoon chopped fresh sage leaves
2 teaspoons kosher salt
½ teaspoon black pepper
Grated zest of 1 lemon
¼ cup olive oil

2 3-pound chickens, giblets and neck removed, or 4 pounds bone-in chicken breasts, rinsed and patted dry

To make the herb and lemon paste: Place the onion, basil, parsley, rosemary, mint, sage, salt, pepper, and lemon zest in a food processor fitted with a steel blade and pulse until coarsely chopped. While the machine is running, gradually add the olive oil in a thin, steady stream and process until the mixture is smooth and emulsified.

Place the chicken in a large glass or ceramic bowl and cover with the paste. Cover and refrigerate for 6 to 8 hours, or overnight. Discard the excess paste.

Preheat the oven to 500 degrees.

Place a large cast-iron skillet over medium-high heat and when it is hot, add the chicken. Cook until deep brown on all sides, about 10 minutes. (You will need to do this in two batches.)

Place the chicken in the oven and roast until the juices run clear from the thigh and the leg moves easily, about 35 minutes (25 minutes if you are roasting breasts only).

TURKEY SCALOPPINE PORTUGUESE-STYLE

I hate veal scaloppine because it doesn't have any taste; I find turkey far more interesting. This slightly spicy and elegant rendition was inspired by trips to Boston's many Portuguese markets. The sauce can also be served over pasta or polenta.

Serve with Apple-Fennel Mashed Potatoes (page 170), Everyday Polenta (page 180), or Chilled Black Olive Spaghetti Salad (page 212).

SERVES 4

SPICE RUB:
2 tablespoons Hungarian paprika
2 teaspoons Dijon mustard
1 teaspoon kosher salt
1 teaspoon black pepper
¼ teaspoon cayenne pepper
2 tablespoons olive oil

¼ cup all-purpose flour
1⅓ pounds turkey thigh cutlets, pounded to ¼ inch thick
3 tablespoons olive oil
1 tablespoon unsalted butter
½ Spanish onion, chopped
2 garlic cloves, thinly sliced
2 chorizo sausages, cut into medium dice
⅓ cup coarsely chopped almonds
6 roasted plum tomatoes (see page 31)
2 cups Chicken Broth (page 38) or canned low-sodium chicken broth
½ large fennel bulb, trimmed, cored and thinly sliced

¼ cup fresh lemon juice (about 1 lemon)
2 to 3 tablespoons chopped fresh cilantro leaves, for garnish
Greens from 1 bunch scallions, thinly sliced, for garnish

To make the rub: Place the paprika, mustard, salt, black pepper, cayenne, and olive oil in a shallow bowl and mix together.

Place the flour on a plate. Dredge the turkey cutlets in the rub and then very lightly in the flour.

Place a large skillet over medium-high heat and when it is hot, add 2 tablespoons of the oil and the butter. Add the turkey cutlets, one at a time, making sure the skillet is hot prior to each addition. Cook until the edges begin to color, about 3 minutes. Turn and cook about 2 minutes on the other side. Remove the turkey to a plate.

Reheat the pan and add the remaining 1 tablespoon oil. Add the onion and garlic and cook for 1 minute. Add the chorizo and almonds and cook for 2 minutes. Add the tomatoes, chicken broth, fennel, and lemon juice, stirring well after each addition. Bring to a low boil.

Return the turkey to the pan and cook until it has completely heated through, about 2 minutes. Garnish with the cilantro and scallions and serve.

Bistro Stuffed Chicken with Spicy Italian Sausage, Fennel, and Red Onions

*T*his is an elegant way to serve chicken with stuffing at any time of the year. The sauce bastes the chicken and imbues it with spicy, sweet, and salty flavors. Your butcher can remove the chicken thigh bone for you. Serve with Everyday Polenta (page 180) or basmati rice.

SERVES 4

4 chicken leg-and-thigh pieces, trimmed of excess fat and
    thigh bone removed
¾ to 1 pound spicy Italian sausages, removed from casings
2 tablespoons all-purpose flour
1 teaspoon kosher salt
1 teaspoon black pepper
1 tablespoon olive oil
2 red onions, thinly sliced
4 garlic cloves, thinly sliced
6 large button mushrooms, trimmed, wiped clean, and thinly sliced
½ to 1 teaspoon crushed red pepper flakes
¼ cup brandy (optional)
1 cup crushed fresh or canned tomatoes, coarsely chopped, including juice
1 cup dry white wine
3 tablespoons balsamic vinegar
3 cups Chicken Broth (page 38) or canned low-sodium chicken broth
5 bay leaves
3 fresh rosemary sprigs
2 tablespoons Dijon mustard

Preheat the oven to 400 degrees.

Stuff each chicken thigh with one quarter of the sausage meat. Fold the skin over and, if necessary, snugly tie a string around each thigh to keep it together.

Combine the flour, salt, and pepper on a plate and lightly dredge each chicken piece in the mixture.

Place a large cast-iron skillet or other heavy ovenproof skillet over medium-high heat and when it is hot, add the oil. Add the chicken pieces, one at a time, skin side down, making sure that the pan is hot prior to each addition.

Scatter the onions, garlic, mushrooms, and red pepper flakes around the chicken. Cook until the chicken is well browned, about 3 to 4 minutes per side.

Add the brandy, if desired, and shake the pan. Add the tomatoes and wine and bring the mixture to a low boil.

Add the vinegar, chicken broth, bay leaves, and rosemary and return to a low boil. Transfer the pan to the oven, and bake until the chicken is tender, about 40 minutes.

Remove the chicken pieces to a plate and set aside. (When the chicken is cool enough to handle, remove the string if necessary.)

Add the mustard to the skillet and bring to a boil over medium-high heat. Lower the heat and simmer until the sauce has reduced by one-third, about 10 minutes. Return the chicken to the skillet, cook until the chicken is heated through, and serve.

PAN-ROASTED BREAST OF CHICKEN GLAZED IN A RHUBARB "AGRODOLCE"

Agrodolce literally means "sour-sweet" in Italian. Based on a classic *agrodolce* recipe, this chicken dish pairs apple cider, orange juice, and brown sugar with sour, rich balsamic vinegar and tart rhubarb. Its clean taste makes it an ideal main course on a warm spring or summer evening.

Serve with Golden Raisin Polenta (page 186).

SERVES 4

2 whole chicken breasts, cut in half
1 teaspoon kosher salt
½ teaspoon black pepper
1 tablespoon olive oil
1 tablespoon chopped peeled fresh ginger
1 Spanish onion, chopped
8 rhubarb stalks, trimmed and cut into small dice
2 tablespoons unsalted butter
1½ cups apple cider
Juice of 1 orange
½ cup balsamic vinegar
1 teaspoon chopped fresh rosemary leaves
1 tablespoon lightly packed light brown sugar

Sprinkle the chicken breasts with the salt and pepper. Place a large skillet over medium-high heat, and when it is hot, add the breasts, skin side down. Cook until browned, about 4 minutes on each side. Transfer the breasts to a plate.

Reheat the pan and add the oil. Add the ginger, onion, and rhubarb, stirring well after each addition, and cook for 5 minutes. Add the butter, cider, orange juice, balsamic vinegar, and rosemary, stirring well after each addition, and bring to a low boil. Cook until reduced by one-half, about 15 minutes.

Add the brown sugar, return the chicken to the pan, and cook until the chicken is tender, about 10 minutes. Serve immediately, in the skillet.

SIMPLE ROASTED CHICKEN FOR TWO

*H*ere's another classic version of roasted chicken, perfect for an intimate dinner for two. Serve with Garlic Mashed Potatoes (page 175) and Arugula Salad with Tomato and Cucumber Juice (page 125).

SERVES 2

1 3-pound chicken, giblets and neck removed, rinsed and patted dry
2 garlic bulbs, cloves separated and peeled
4 fresh rosemary sprigs
1 teaspoon kosher salt
1 teaspoon black pepper
1 tablespoon olive oil

SAUCE:
¾ cup dry white wine
3 to 4 tablespoons fresh lemon juice (about 1 lemon)
1 tablespoon brandy (optional)
2 cups Chicken Broth (page 38) or canned low-sodium chicken broth
2 tablespoons chopped fresh flat-leaf parsley leaves
½ teaspoon kosher salt
¼ teaspoon black pepper

Preheat the oven to 400 degrees.

Fill the chicken cavity with the garlic and rosemary. Rub the skin and flesh with the salt and pepper.

Place a large cast-iron skillet or other heavy ovenproof skillet over medium-high heat and when it is hot, add the oil. Add the chicken, breast side down, and brown it on all sides, about 10 minutes. Discard any fat that remains in the pan, reserving the juices in the pan.

Transfer the pan to the oven and roast until the juices run clear from the thigh and the leg moves easily, about 35 minutes.

Remove the chicken to a plate. Remove the garlic and rosemary from the chicken and set aside.

To make the sauce: Pour off half the pan juices from the skillet and return the skillet to medium-high heat. Add the reserved garlic and rosemary and cook for 2 minutes. Add the wine, lemon juice, brandy, if desired, and chicken broth and cook until the garlic is soft, about 12 to 15 minutes.

Discard 3 of the rosemary sprigs. Remove the leaves from the remaining rosemary sprig and return to the sauce. Transfer the sauce to a blender and puree.

Return the sauce to the skillet and bring to a boil over high heat. Cut the chicken in half through the backbone, cut out the backbone, return the chicken to the skillet, and warm it through. Add the parsley, salt, and pepper and serve.

QUICK DUCK CONFIT

*C*onfit is a method for preserving meat in its own rendered fat, created before refrigerators and freezers were around. Traditionally, the meat is covered overnight with salt and sometimes spices. After slow cooking, the meat is placed in an earthenware crock, where the fat then solidifies and forms an air-tight seal around the meat. It is then stored for six months to one year, on a shelf.

Either way, this dish is unbelievably succulent, proving the old saw, "Where there is fat there is flavor." Serve with creamed corn and peach chutney.

SERVES 4

4 duck legs
1 tablespoon kosher salt
1 tablespoon black pepper
2 to 3 fresh rosemary sprigs
3 bay leaves
2½ cups duck fat, vegetable oil, or chicken fat

Preheat the oven to 250 degrees.

Place the duck legs, salt, pepper, rosemary, bay leaves, and duck fat in a large ovenproof skillet and bring to a low simmer over medium-high heat.

Transfer to the oven and cook until the meat is falling off the bones, about 3½ to 4 hours.

Serve immediately.

OLIVES SPECIAL DRY-RUBBED ROAST DUCK

I love eating old-fashioned crispy roast duck skin that has been rendered of its fat. Our recipe is based on the classic French confit; it will never be part of a low-fat diet, but it's worth the occasional indulgence. If you're feeling guilty about using duck fat, olive oil is an acceptable substitute.

Serve with Golden Raisin Polenta (page 186) or Black Truffle, Potato, and Parsnip "Risotto" (page 164).

SERVES 2

DRY RUB:
¼ teaspoon crushed red pepper flakes
¼ teaspoon ground coriander
1 teaspoon chopped fresh thyme leaves
1 teaspoon kosher salt
1 teaspoon black pepper
1 teaspoon dried fennel seeds
½ teaspoon ground ginger

1 5½- to 6-pound duck, split in half down the back and backbone
    removed, duck flattened
About 4 cups rendered duck fat (see mail-order sources, page 351),
    at room temperature

To make the dry rub: Combine the pepper flakes, coriander, thyme, salt, pepper, fennel, and ginger in a small bowl. Rub it into both sides of the duck. Cover and refrigerate for 4 hours, or overnight.

Preheat the oven to 225 degrees.

Place the duck in a cast-iron skillet or other heavy ovenproof skillet and cover with the duck fat. Bring to a gentle simmer over medium heat. Place in the oven and cook, uncovered, until the meat is almost falling off the bone, about 3½ to 4 hours.

Carefully remove the duck, using a spatula, and set aside. Drain off half the fat and place the skillet over medium-high heat. When the fat is very hot, add the duck, skin side down, and cook until it is golden brown, about 3 minutes. Drain on a brown paper bag or paper towels and serve immediately.

(The remaining fat or oil may be strained and reused. It will keep covered in the refrigerator for up to 2 weeks. It can be used for sautéing or for rubbing on potatoes to be roasted.)

Pan-Fried Cornmeal-and-Cumin-Rubbed Cornish Game Hens

*W*hen I was a child growing up in the South, my mother used to take us to a little place around the corner that specialized in cornmeal-fried chicken. And cornmeal-fried okra. And cornmeal-fried tomatoes. I loved it all then and I love it still, particularly the addition of the cumin, an idea I got after one of my cooks described eating a cumin-scented dish on a vacation in Greece. It's a perfect complement to the rich flavor of game hens. If you love cumin, you'll love this. If you don't, omit it, and enjoy this dish anyway.

Perfect served hot, at room temperature, or chilled. Take this to a tailgate party or picnic and serve it over Arugula Salad with Tomato and Cucumber Juice (page 125).

SERVES 4

2 tablespoons chopped fresh cilantro leaves
2 tablespoons chopped scallions
1 tablespoon chopped peeled fresh ginger
2 large eggs, lightly beaten
2 heaping tablespoons ground cumin
⅔ cup stone-ground yellow cornmeal
⅓ cup all-purpose flour
1 teaspoon kosher salt
½ teaspoon black pepper
4 14-ounce Cornish game hens, butterflied and backbone removed
2 tablespoons olive oil

Preheat the oven to 375 degrees.

Place the cilantro, scallions, and ginger on a large plate and mix together.

Place the eggs in a shallow bowl.

Combine the cumin, cornmeal, flour, salt, and pepper on another large plate.

Dip the hens in the cilantro mixture, then in the eggs, and then in the cornmeal mixture.

Place a large skillet over medium-high heat and when it is hot, add the oil. Add the hens and cook one at a time, until they are golden brown, about 4 minutes each. Put the hens in a large baking pan in the oven and cook until they are deep brown and completely cooked, about 15 minutes.

RABBIT AGRODOLCE (SWEET-AND-SOUR RABBIT)

*O*ne of my fondest memories is of a dish I had in Tuscany called Sweet-and-Sour Rabbit. I've always loved the combination of the twang of the sour, the spice of the pepper, and the sweet of the honey. You can, of course, substitute chicken. Serve this with basmati rice.

SERVES 4 TO 6

2 tablespoons olive oil
2 3-pound rabbits, cut into serving pieces
1 teaspoon kosher salt
1 teaspoon black pepper
5 garlic cloves, thinly sliced
1½ tablespoons chopped peeled fresh ginger
½ pound smoked ham, cut into thick strips
1 teaspoon crushed red pepper flakes
3 to 4 red onions, thinly sliced
1 fennel bulb, trimmed, cored, and thinly sliced
1 Scotch bonnet or jalapeño pepper, chopped
⅓ cup white sugar
1¾ cups fresh orange juice
1 cup balsamic vinegar
⅓ cup honey
1 cup Chicken Broth (page 38) or canned low-sodium chicken broth
1 heaping tablespoon Dijon mustard
1 bunch scallions, half trimmed and left whole, half chopped
*   (white and green parts)*
¼ cup chopped fresh cilantro leaves
4 tablespoons unsalted butter (optional)
1 teaspoon toasted sesame oil (optional)

Place a large skillet over medium-high heat and when it is hot, add the oil. Sprinkle the rabbit with the salt and pepper, add it to the pan, skin side down, and cook until golden brown, about 5 minutes per side. Transfer the rabbit to a plate and reheat the pan.

Add the garlic, ginger, and ham and cook for 2 minutes. Add the crushed red pepper flakes, onions, and fennel, stirring well after each addition, and cook until the vegetables are light golden brown, about 10 minutes.

Add the rabbit, Scotch bonnet, sugar, orange juice, vinegar, honey, chicken broth, and mustard, stirring well after each addition, and cook for 5 minutes. Reduce the heat to low, cover, and cook until the mixture is thickened and reduced to a glaze and the rabbit is tender, about 1 hour. Add the whole and chopped scallions, the cilantro, and, if desired, the butter and sesame oil.

QUAIL CACCIATORE

Cacciatore means "hunter-style" in Italian, and the deep flavors of the sauce are well suited to dark-fleshed game birds.

Although I'm a big fan of eating squab, I'm not generally fond of cooking small birds. I do like this preparation, however, because it seems to eliminate the threat of overcooking the tiny quail. Rich and elegant, Quail Cacciatore is a great dish for the late fall.

You can substitute equal amounts of chicken or turkey parts for the quail.

Serve with Everyday Polenta (page 180) or Toasted Corn Polenta (page 188).

SERVES 4

8 quail, backbone removed and quail butterflied
1 teaspoon kosher salt
1 teaspoon black pepper
2 tablespoons olive oil
½ cup chopped slab bacon or chopped high-quality thick-sliced lean bacon
4 anchovy fillets, minced
4 shallots, minced
24 chanterelles or other mushrooms, trimmed, wiped clean, and halved
8 garlic cloves, thinly sliced
6 fresh or canned tomatoes, diced
2 cups Dark Stock (page 40), made with veal bones, or Chicken Broth
*   (page 38), or canned low-sodium chicken broth*
2 cups dry white wine
½ cup balsamic vinegar
2 tablespoons chopped fresh rosemary leaves

Sprinkle the quail with the salt and pepper. Place a large skillet over medium-high heat and when it is very hot, add the oil. Add the quail, skin side down, and cook for 3 minutes. Add the bacon and cook until the quail is browned, about 4 minutes on each side. Transfer the quail to a platter. Drain off the bacon fat and reheat the skillet.

Add the anchovies, shallots, chanterelles, and garlic and cook until the shallots and garlic are beginning to caramelize, about 7 minutes. Add the tomatoes, veal stock, wine, vinegar, and rosemary and cook for 15 minutes. Return the quail to the pan and cook until the quail is heated through, about 2 to 3 minutes.

GINGER MUSTARD CHICKEN

*M*any of the recipes in this book are meant to be eaten on special occasions, but this is the kind of dish I eat at home with Olivia and our brood. Easy to prepare and low in fat, it's an ideal weekday dinner.

Serve with Arugula Salad with Tomato and Cucumber Juice (page 125).

SERVES 4

1 tablespoon chopped peeled fresh ginger
3 garlic cloves, minced
1 tablespoon Dijon mustard
2 whole skinless, boneless chicken breasts, split
1 to 2 medium beefsteak tomatoes, cut into 8 slices total
1 teaspoon kosher salt
1 teaspoon black pepper
¼ cup fresh bread crumbs
1 teaspoon chopped fresh flat-leaf parsley leaves
1 teaspoon chopped fresh rosemary leaves

Preheat the oven to 400 degrees.

Place the ginger, garlic, and mustard in a small bowl and mash together with a fork to form a paste.

Place the chicken in a baking dish and coat the top of the chicken breasts with the ginger mixture. Top with the tomato slices. Sprinkle with the salt, pepper, bread crumbs, parsley, and rosemary, place in the oven, and bake until tender, about 15 minutes.

MEATS ▪

PAN-ROASTED RIB EYE WITH GORGONZOLA VIDALIA ONIONS

For years I stopped serving beef because a) I got bored with cooking it and b) our customers were either too bored or too afraid to eat it. Things came full circle, as they always do, and once again it has become part of my repertoire. I always joke that when Olives' tenure is done, I'll convert it into a steakhouse, with this dish as the star attraction.

Like foie gras, this shamelessly rich dish is one of the great indulgences, best saved for special occasions.

Rib eye of beef, also known as prime rib, is a boneless cut from the rib portion. You can substitute New York strip steak.

SERVES 4

GORGONZOLA VIDALIA ONIONS:
2 tablespoons unsalted butter
1 recipe Roasted Vidalia Onions (page 30) (you can substitute any sweet
white onion), thinly sliced
½ cup chopped smoked ham
1 cup heavy cream
2 teaspoons chopped fresh rosemary leaves
2 tablespoons scallion greens
⅓ cup crumbled Gorgonzola cheese

1 tablespoon olive oil
4 10-ounce rib-eye steaks
1 teaspoon kosher salt
1 teaspoon black pepper

To make the onions: Place a large skillet over medium heat and when it is hot, add the butter, onions, and ham, stirring well after each addition. Cook until lightly caramelized, about 8 minutes.

Add the cream, rosemary, and scallions, stirring well after each addition, and cook until the mixture begins to reduce, about 5 minutes.

Meanwhile, place a large cast-iron skillet over medium-high heat and when it is hot, add the oil. Sprinkle the steaks with the salt and pepper. Add the steaks to the pan and cook for about 4 to 5 minutes on each side for medium-rare.

Add the Gorgonzola cheese to the onion mixture and cook until just heated through.

Slice the steaks on the bias and serve on top of the Gorgonzola onions.

Pan-Griddled Surf-and-Turf Rib-Eye Steak for Two

When I was a child, I used to love going to old steakhouses and ordering surf and turf; I still love it.

I swear I'm not a fusion cook: this is another recipe inspired by Carl's Pagoda, one of my favorite Chinatown restaurants.

Char the steak for a smoky flavor and crunchy texture. You can also grill the steak. Serve with Garlic-Roasted Radicchio (page 137) and Carrot Mashed Potatoes (page 176).

SERVES 2

■ *There are two schools of thought as to whether meats should be cooked at room temperature or just out of the refrigerator. I've found meat cooks more evenly when at room temperature but you get a better char if it's chilled because you can smoke it more. What do I think? Unless you have incredible ventilation at home, leave the chilled meat for restaurants.*

1 tablespoon olive oil
1 14- to 16-ounce rib-eye steak or boneless sirloin steak
1¼ teaspoons kosher salt
1¼ teaspoons black pepper

SAUCE:
2 tablespoons chopped slab bacon or chopped high-quality
*   thick-sliced lean bacon*
3 garlic cloves, thinly sliced
1 large shallot, thinly sliced

1 teaspoon grated peeled fresh ginger
½ cup balsamic vinegar
¼ cup soy sauce
1 tablespoon white sugar
½ cup water

2 teaspoons unsalted butter
6 large shrimp, peeled and deveined
⅛ teaspoon toasted sesame oil
2 scallions, finely chopped, white and green parts, for garnish
6 fresh cilantro sprigs, for garnish

Place a large cast-iron skillet over medium-high heat and when it is hot, add the oil. Sprinkle the steak with 1 teaspoon each of the salt and pepper. Add the steak and set another cast-iron skillet or a heavy pot on top of the steak to help it cook consistently through. Cook for about 4 to 5 minutes on each side. Remove the steak and set it aside.

To make the sauce: Reheat the pan over medium heat. When it is hot, add the bacon, garlic, shallot, and ginger, stirring well after each addition, and cook for 3 minutes. Add the vinegar, soy sauce, sugar, and water, stirring well after each addition, and bring to a low boil. Cook until the mixture becomes syrupy, about 7 minutes.

In the meantime, melt the butter in a medium-size skillet over a medium-high heat. Sprinkle the shrimp with the remaining ¼ teaspoon each salt and pepper. Add the shrimp to the skillet. Cook until it is pink and opaque throughout, about 3 minutes. Add the shrimp and sesame oil to the sauce.

Slice the steak on the diagonal, arrange on a platter, and pour the sauce over it. Sprinkle with the scallions and cilantro sprigs and serve.

BROOKLYN PORTERHOUSE WITH CILANTRO MARINADE

"*Brooklyn porterhouse*" is a term that the meat packers in the old Jewish sections of New York used for skirt steak in the early twenties. I can be sure they didn't use this heady marinade for what is one of my favorite cuts.

SERVES 4

CILANTRO MARINADE:
2 roasted garlic cloves (see page 28), peeled
1 tablespoon Dijon mustard
¼ cup chopped fresh cilantro leaves
Grated zest of ½ lemon
2 tablespoons balsamic vinegar
2 tablespoons olive oil

1½ to 2 pounds skirt or flank steak
1 teaspoon kosher salt
½ teaspoon black pepper

To make the cilantro marinade: Place the roasted garlic, mustard, cilantro, lemon zest, balsamic vinegar, and oil in a large shallow glass or ceramic bowl and mash to a paste.

Place the steak in the marinade. Cover and refrigerate at least 8 hours or overnight, turning occasionally.

Prepare the grill or preheat the broiler.

Remove the steak from the marinade, reserving the marinade. Sprinkle both sides of the steak with the salt and pepper. Grill or broil for about 5 minutes per side for medium-rare, basting occasionally with the reserved marinade.

Thinly slice on the diagonal and serve.

WHOLE ROASTED GARLIC-STUDDED RACK OF VEAL

*S*erve this impressive dish for a truly elegant occasion when you're not concerned about your budget. Roasting the whole rack is the most succulent and delicious way to serve veal.

Serve with Black Truffle, Potato, and Parsnip "Risotto" (page 164) or Asparagus Risotto with Ragù of Crazy Mushrooms (page 193) and Garlic-Roasted Radicchio (page 137).

SERVES 4

1 4½-pound rack of veal
6 to 8 garlic cloves, cut into eighths
¼ cup fresh rosemary leaves
¼ cup fresh thyme leaves
¼ cup fresh basil leaves
Grated zest of 1 orange
1 teaspoon kosher salt
½ teaspoon black pepper
½ cup olive oil

Place the veal on a platter and make holes all over it about an inch apart, by pushing a paring knife into the fat and turning it. Insert a garlic sliver into each hole.

Place the remaining garlic, the rosemary, thyme, basil, orange zest, salt, and pepper in a food processor fitted with a steel blade and pulse until finely chopped. Add the olive oil and process until the mixture forms a chunky paste.

Rub the mixture all over the veal. Cover and refrigerate for at least 2 hours, or overnight.

Preheat the oven to 425 degrees or prepare the grill.

Roast or grill the veal, uncovered, for about 25 minutes.

Let the meat rest for 15 to 20 minutes. Carve one bone per person.

OSSO BUCO OF VEAL

*V*eal shanks are another one of those economical cuts of meat that the Italians raised to a culinary pinnacle. At Olives, we take a lot of pride in our Osso Buco of Veal. It blends hearty rustic and soulful flavors with a light, ethereal texture that melts in your mouth. We slow-roast the whole shank, which Northern Italians call *stinco di vitello*.

This is a hearty but elegant dish that is perfect for a small dinner party in the winter. It's rich and flavorful, like a stew, except that the meat remains on the bone. Serve with basmati rice, Everyday Polenta (page 180) or Garlic Mashed Potatoes (page 175) and grilled asparagus.

SERVES 4

¼ cup all-purpose flour

1 teaspoon kosher salt

½ teaspoon black pepper

4 14-ounce veal shanks, cut 1½ to 2 inches thick

2 tablespoons olive oil

1 cup chopped slab bacon or chopped high-qulaity thick-sliced lean bacon

6 garlic cloves, thinly sliced

1 Spanish onion, diced

2 large carrots, peeled and diced

3 stalks celery, cut into medium dice

2 leeks (white part only), well washed and chopped

2 cups roughly chopped shiitake mushrooms

2 tablespoons chopped fresh rosemary leaves

1 teaspoon dried fennel seeds

½ teaspoon crushed red pepper flakes

¾ cup dry white wine

½ cup good-quality dry sherry, such as Tio Pepe

4 cups Chicken Broth (page 38), Dark Stock made with veal bones (page 40), or canned low-sodium chicken broth
Finely grated zest of 1 orange
2 tablespoons Dijon mustard
2 tablespoons chopped fresh flat-leaf parsley leaves, for garnish

Preheat the oven to 425 degrees.

Combine the flour, salt, and pepper on a large plate and lightly dust the veal shanks with the mixture.

Place a 14-inch straight-sided ovenproof sauté pan or a 3-to-4-quart Dutch oven over medium-high heat and when it is hot, add the oil. Add the veal shanks and cook until they are deeply golden on the bottom, about 5 minutes. Turn over and cook for about 2 minutes on the second side. Transfer the veal shanks to a plate.

Add the bacon to the pan and cook until it begins to render its fat, about 2 minutes. Add the garlic, onion, carrots, celery, leeks, mushrooms, rosemary, fennel seeds, and pepper flakes, stirring well after each addition, and cook for 10 minutes.

Return the shanks to the pan and add the wine and sherry. Spoon the vegetables over the veal and cook for 5 minutes.

Add the chicken broth and orange zest and bring to a low simmer. Cover and transfer to the oven. Roast for 2 hours.

Transfer the shanks to a plate and return the pan to medium-high heat. Add the mustard and simmer for 10 minutes. Return the shanks to the pan and cook until heated through.

Serve immediately. Garnish with the parsley.

PORK CHOPS AU POIVRE WITH APPLE AND LEEK PUREE

$\mathcal{I}$'m a pepper fanatic. This dish was inspired by the classic Steak au Poivre, but I think that pork works even better because it seems to absorb and carry the pepper flavor better. The apple and leek puree adds just the right counter-balance of sweet and tart.

Pork chops were a staple in my diet growing up, whether served pan-fried with gravy by my mother or braised with tomato sauce by my grand-mother. I use the rib eye, which is more consistently tender, rather than the loin chop. I still love them but rarely order them in a restaurant—unless it's the killer chop cooked by my friend Emeril Lagasse at his restaurant, Emeril's, in New Orleans. He's the only one I know who serves it the way I like it: double-thick, tender, juicy, and spicy.

SERVES 4

APPLE AND LEEK PUREE:
1 tablespoon olive oil
1 leek, well washed and thinly sliced
2 McIntosh apples, peeled, quartered, and thinly sliced
2 tablespoons honey
¼ cup fresh lemon juice (about 1 lemon)
¼ teaspoon ground coriander
1 cinnamon stick

3 tablespoons coarsely cracked black pepper
1½ tablespoons fennel seeds, coarsely chopped
4 6-ounce double-thick rib-eye pork chops, trimmed of fat, brined if
*   desired (see instructions at end of recipe)*
1 tablespoon olive oil
1 tablespoon chopped fresh rosemary leaves

Preheat the oven to 425 degrees.

To make the apple and leek puree: Place a large skillet over medium heat and when it is hot, add the 1 tablespoon oil. Add the leek, apples, honey, lemon juice, coriander, and cinnamon stick, stirring well after each addition, and cook until the leeks and apples are very soft, about 7 minutes. Remove the cinnamon stick, transfer the mixture to a blender, and puree.

Combine the pepper and fennel seeds on a large plate.

If you brined the pork chops (see below), pat them dry. Lightly rub the pork chops with some of the oil and then coat with the pepper-and-fennel mixture.

Place a large ovenproof skillet over medium-high heat and when it is hot, add the remaining 1 tablespoon oil. Add the chops and cook until they are well browned, about 3 minutes on each side. Transfer to the oven and bake until they are firm to the touch, about 12 to 15 minutes.

Reheat the puree, if necessary. Divide it among four plates and top with the pork chops. Sprinkle with the rosemary.

■ *At Olives we brine pork chops before we cook them. Brining is a great method for tenderizing and flavoring meats, especially pork. This is an easy method and even though it's not necessary to brine the pork chops for this dish, in case you're feeling inspired and adventurous and organized, here's the recipe. The pork should be brined two to four days in advance.*

> *3 cups water*
> *1 teaspoon kosher salt*
> *1 cup honey*
> *½ cup lightly packed brown sugar*
> *2 tablespoons black peppercorns*
> *1 bunch fresh rosemary*

1 garlic bulb, unpeeled, sliced crosswise in half

1 Spanish onion, thinly sliced

1 bay leaf

1 tablespoon mustard seeds

Pinch of ground nutmeg

Place the water, salt, honey, brown sugar, peppercorns, rosemary, garlic, onion, bay leaf, mustard seeds, and nutmeg in a large pot and bring to a boil over high heat. Let cool.

Transfer the brine to a large glass or ceramic bowl and add the pork chops, making sure they are completely submerged. Cover and refrigerate for 2 to 4 days.

Remove the pork chops from the brine and discard the brine.

BBQ Slow-Roasted Suckling Pig with Ginger-Honey Glaze

I have had the great fortune to travel almost all over the world, and wherever I go, there is a ceremony around roasting pig. In French Polynesia, on the island of Mooréa, pigs are buried in a pit lined with stone and wrapped in banana leaves. In Spain, they are slow-roasted in brick ovens for hours. In the southern United States, they are barbecued all night. This is obviously not a spur-of-the-moment dish; you'll have to special-order the pig from your butcher and have him prep it.

The New Braunsfels Smoker Company (800-232-3398) makes a great smoker-grill. It helps if your grill or smoker has a thermometer.

Serve with Creamed Corn (page 133) and Arugula Salad with Tomato and Cucumber Juice (page 125) or, if it's winter, any of the fruit polentas.

SERVES 8 TO 10

1 15- to 20-pound suckling pig, butterflied open

GINGER-HONEY GLAZE:
½ cup finely chopped peeled fresh ginger
3 bunches scallions, finely chopped
10 garlic cloves, finely chopped
1 small onion, finely chopped
1 cup honey
½ cup soy sauce
¼ cup toasted sesame oil
2 star anise
½ cup lightly packed brown sugar
½ cup Vietnamese chili garlic sauce
¼ cup finely chopped fresh cilantro leaves

To make the glaze: Combine all the ingredients in a medium-size bowl. Place the pig on a large platter or in a nonreactive baking pan and pour half the glaze over the pig. Cover and refrigerate the pig and the remaining glaze.

Prepare the grill 2 hours ahead of time. Have a small bucket of water ready in case you need to tame the fire, and add more fuel if the fire starts to burn out.

The grill is ready when the temperature reaches 200 to 225 degrees, or when you can hold your hand 12 to 14 inches above the bed of charcoal for three counts. The embers should have a light glow.

Discard the glaze used to marinate the pig. Place the pig on the grill, skin side up. Cover, sit back, and have a cold beer. When you are finished with the beer, go check the pig to be sure there are no flare-ups from the dripping fat. If there are, douse with a small amount of water. Cover the grill again and return to your seat. Check every 15 minutes or so; always replace the cover.

After 3½ hours, baste the pig with the reserved glaze. After another 30 minutes or so, the skin should be crispy, sticky, and caramelized and the pig should be ready to eat. Place the remaining glaze in a small pot and cook until warm. Transfer to a bowl and serve alongside the pig as a sauce.

GINGERED SLOW-BRAISED LAMB SHANKS

Braised lamb shanks are the foundation for much of the cooking at Olives and used as the base when making many sauces. When braised correctly, the meat should be almost falling off the bone and be silky in texture. The meat will have a very distinctive flavor: a slightly gamey edge like sirloin steak but spicy and more intense, supple, and tender. You may need to order these in advance from your butcher.

Serve these over Apple-Fennel Mashed Potatoes (page 170).

SERVES 4

¼ cup olive oil

4 12-ounce domestic hind bone-in lamb shanks

1½ teaspoons kosher salt

1¼ teaspoons black pepper

1 anchovy fillet, minced

2 tablespoons chopped peeled fresh ginger

8 garlic cloves, thinly sliced

1 fennel bulb, trimmed, cored, and thinly sliced

1 Spanish onion, thinly sliced

½ teaspoon fennel seeds

¾ teaspoon crushed red pepper flakes

2 teaspoons ground cumin

⅔ cup dry red wine

1 cup balsamic vinegar

3 roasted tomatoes (see page 31)

½ cup cooked chick peas, rinsed

3 fresh rosemary sprigs

10 cups water, or Dark Stock (page 40),
Chicken Broth (page 38),
or canned low-sodium chicken broth

Place a large cast-iron skillet or other heavy ovenproof skillet or a Dutch oven over medium-high heat and when it is hot, add 2 tablespoons of the oil. Sprinkle the lamb shanks with 1 teaspoon of the salt and 1 teaspoon of the pepper and add them to the pan. Cook until they are browned on both sides, about 4 to 5 minutes on each side. Set the shanks aside and discard the oil.

Wipe the skillet clean and reheat it. Add the remaining 2 tablespoons oil. Add the anchovy fillet, ginger, and garlic, stirring well after each addition, and cook until the garlic is golden, about 3 minutes. Add the fennel, onion, fennel seeds, pepper flakes, cumin, the remaining ½ teaspoon salt and ¼ teaspoon pepper, the wine, and vinegar, stirring well after each addition. Cook until the sauce has reduced somewhat, about 5 minutes.

Add the tomatoes and chick peas and return the shanks to the pan. Add the rosemary and water, bring to a simmer, and transfer the skillet to the oven.

Bake, uncovered, until the meat is falling off the bone, about 3 hours. Transfer to 4 plates or a large serving platter.

MOUNTAIN LAMB SCALOPPINE WITH FIGS AND HONEY

*T*his is an unusual way to prepare lamb and one of my favorites. I saw the pairing of lamb and honey on the menu in a restaurant in the French Alps; I didn't get to eat it but I could taste it in my mind. When I got home I experimented with the combination; adding the sweet rich figs seemed natural. The small amount of mustard is critical; it smooths out the sauce and takes the edge off the vinegar.

When you start cooking, you might think that this looks like a huge amount of lamb. It isn't: it shrinks as it cooks. Serve with basmati rice.

■ *It's important to buy very lean lamb, and not the part with sinews. Ask the butcher to cut it from the top round. And be sure not to overcook it—leave it medium-rare.*

SERVES 4

FENNEL RUB:
2 tablespoons fennel seeds
1 tablespoon ground ginger
2 teaspoons kosher salt
2 teaspoons black pepper
½ cup all-purpose flour

1 tablespoon olive oil
1½ pounds lamb leg, cut into cutlets, scored, and pounded
*   to ¼-inch thickness*

FIG SAUCE:
1¼ cups water
1 cup dried Black Mission figs, quartered
Juice of 2 oranges
1 tablespoon chopped peeled fresh ginger
½ cup honey
¼ cup balsamic vinegar
4 bay leaves
2 teaspoons chopped fresh thyme leaves, plus 2 whole sprigs for garnish
1 teaspoon toasted sesame oil
2 teaspoons Dijon mustard
2 tablespoons unsalted butter (optional)

To make the fennel rub: Place the fennel seeds, ginger, salt, and pepper in a blender and blend until it forms a fine powder. Add the flour and place the mixture on a large plate.

Place a large cast-iron pan over medium-high heat and when it is smoking hot, add the olive oil. Dredge the lamb in the rub and add it to the pan, one piece at a time, making sure that the pan is hot prior to each addition and cooking in batches, if necessary. Cook until the edges begin to color, about 2 to 3 minutes on each side. Remove the lamb from the pan and set aside.

To make the sauce: Add the water, figs, and orange juice to the pan and bring to a boil over medium-high heat. Cook until the figs have softened and are plump, about 10 minutes. Add the ginger, honey, vinegar, bay leaves, thyme, and sesame oil, stirring well after each addition, and cook until the mixture is reduced and syrupy, about 10 minutes.

Remove the bay leaves and add the mustard and, if desired, the butter. Return the lamb to the pan and cook until the lamb is just heated through, about 1 minute. Serve immediately.

OLIVES MARINATED LEG OF LAMB SANDWICH ON OLIVE BRUSCHETTA

*T*his is a signature dish that Paul O'Connell, my first chef, and I came up with. We wanted something interesting but relatively simple. The spice paste is a great way to add seasoning and sweetness to the lamb, and it's also good on flank steak.

This is a perfect summertime barbecue or Super Bowl or Sunday lunch dish.

SERVES 12, 2 OPEN-FACED SANDWICHES EACH

SPICE PASTE:
½ cup Hungarian paprika
¼ cup ground cumin
¼ cup chopped fresh rosemary leaves or 1½ tablespoons dried rosemary
2 tablespoons turmeric
½ teaspoon ground cinnamon
1 teaspoon cayenne pepper
¼ teaspoon ground nutmeg
8 garlic cloves, finely chopped
1 cup extra-virgin olive oil

6 pounds boneless lamb leg, butterflied open

24 slices hearty bread
1 cup Black Olive Paste (page 46) or store-bought
    (San Remo brand is good)

To make the spice paste: Place the paprika, cumin, rosemary, turmeric, cinnamon, cayenne, nutmeg, and garlic cloves in a food processor fitted with a steel blade and pulse five times. While the machine is running, gradually add the olive oil in a thin, steady stream and process until emulsified.

Place the lamb leg in a large mixing bowl and cover with the spice paste. Cover and refrigerate for 6 to 8 hours, or overnight.

Prepare the grill.

Pound the thickest part of the lamb until it is of uniform thickness and place on the grill, fat side down. Cook, uncovered, for 18 to 20 minutes. Turn over and cook, covered, for 15 to 20 minutes. The outside should be charred and the inside still pink; some parts will be rarer than others. Transfer to a platter, cover with aluminum foil, and let rest for 5 to 10 minutes before slicing.

While the lamb is resting, place the bread on the grill and cook until it is browned on both sides.

Slice the lamb against the grain. Spread the bread with olive paste and top with the sliced lamb. Serve immediately.

FISH ·

Scallops with Chestnuts and Oranges

About the time scallop season opens in November, chestnuts are also hitting their prime. Serve this with Creamy Chestnut Risotto (page 203).

SERVES 4

¼ cup chestnut flour (available in specialty food stores or by mail-order—
    see page 351)
1 teaspoon kosher salt
¼ teaspoon black pepper
1 pound bay scallops
1 tablespoon olive oil
1 teaspoon unsalted butter
8 fresh, frozen, or canned chestnuts (cooked as described on page 204),
    shelled and finely chopped
1 tablespoon chopped fresh flat-leaf parsley leaves
½ cup fresh orange juice
½ cup Chicken Broth (page 38), or canned low-sodium chicken broth
1 orange, peeled and divided into segments and cut from membranes

In a small bowl, mix together the chestnut flour, salt, and pepper. Place the scallops on a large plate and sprinkle with the flour mixture.

Place a large skillet over medium-high heat and when it is hot, add the oil. Add the scallops and cook until deeply browned on all sides, about 1 to 2 minutes per side. Transfer the scallops to a plate.

Wipe the skillet clean. Melt the butter over medium heat. Add the chestnuts and parsley and cook until the chestnuts are browned, about 2 minutes. Add the orange juice and broth and cook until the sauce reduces and begins to thicken, about 2 minutes.

Return the scallops to the sauce, add the orange segments, and cook for 1 minute. Serve immediately.

GRILLED SCALLOPS WITH WALNUT BUTTER PASTE

*O*ne of the true pleasures of living in New England is the vastness of the quality resources available from the sea. Fresh bay boat scallops are among the reasons I love living here.

You can get rosemary branches at a good produce market. If they're not available, use bamboo skewers, soaked for 15 minutes in water.

The walnut butter paste is also good on grilled lamb chops, chicken, or salmon. Serve this on Shaved Raw Fennel and Red Onion Salad (page 121).

SERVES 4 TO 6

20 jumbo sea scallops (about 2 pounds)
2 garlic cloves, minced
Grated zest of ½ lemon
2 tablespoons olive oil
1 tablespoon chopped fresh basil leaves
1 tablespoon chopped fresh rosemary leaves
1 tablespoon chopped fresh parsley leaves

WALNUT BUTTER PASTE:
1 cup toasted walnuts
1 teaspoon chopped peeled fresh ginger
½ cup water
¼ cup fresh lemon juice (about 1 lemon)
½ cup olive oil
1 tablespoon balsamic vinegar
1 tablespoon chopped fresh flat-leaf parsley leaves
4 large fresh rosemary sprigs, leaves removed from the bottom three
*   quarters of each sprig*

Place the scallops in a large glass or ceramic bowl and toss with the garlic, lemon zest, olive oil, basil, rosemary, and parsley. Cover and refrigerate for 3 hours.

To make the walnut butter paste: Place the walnuts, ginger, water, and lemon juice in the bowl of a food processor fitted with a steel blade and process until the mixture forms a paste. Add the olive oil, vinegar, and parsley and process until the paste has a creamy consistency, about 2 minutes. Set aside.

Prepare the grill.

Thread 5 scallops onto each rosemary branch and place on the grill. Cook until just opaque, about 2 to 3 minutes per side. Transfer to a serving platter and drizzle with the walnut butter paste. Serve immediately.

OCEAN ROCKFISH POACHED IN SPICES AND STOCK

*R*ubbing a seasoning paste into fish is a great alternative to marinating and intensifies flavor without adding any fat. You can substitute striped bass or perch for the rockfish.

SERVES 4

SEASONING PASTE:
1 tablespoon olive oil
2 garlic cloves, minced
2 anchovy fillets, minced
1 tablespoon chopped black olives
1 tablespoon chopped capers
1 teaspoon ground cumin
1 teaspoon turmeric
½ teaspoon cayenne pepper
⅛ teaspoon ground coriander
Pinch of ground nutmeg

2 pounds rockfish fillets
1½ to 2 cups Dark Stock (page 40) or canned low-sodium chicken broth
2 tablespoons chopped fresh flat-leaf parsley leaves

To make the seasoning paste: Place a large skillet over medium-high heat and when it is hot, add the oil. Add the garlic, anchovy fillets, olives, and capers, stirring well after each addition, and cook for 2 minutes. Add the cumin, turmeric, cayenne, coriander, and nutmeg, stirring well after each addition, and cook for 1 minute. Remove from the heat, and when it is cool, rub the paste into the fish.

Reheat the skillet and add the fish, skin side down, and cook until it is seared, about 2 minutes. Add 1½ cups of the stock, bring to a simmer, and cook for 5 to 6 minutes, basting the fish every few minutes with the cooking liquid. Add up to ½ cup more stock if necessary. Turn the fish over and cook for about 4 minutes, basting every few minutes.

Transfer the fish to a large platter and spoon the sauce around it. Garnish with the chopped parsley and serve immediately.

Mussels with Moroccan Spices and Chick Peas

I am a big fan of mussels, especially now that the technology of farming them has made them safer, cleaner, and more consistent in size and flavor. This is one case where farming fish has actually improved the product. Rich in iron, vitamin C, and niacin, mussels are also high in protein and low in fat. They are especially wonderful steamed in white wine. When you want something more complex, try this spice-and-chick-pea combination, which adds substance and backbone to the sweet, musty aroma of the mussels.

This is a great first course for Mountain Lamb Scaloppine (page 274), or simply served for lunch, with bread and a Pinot Grigio, which will stand up well to the spiciness.

SERVES 3 TO 4 AS AN ENTRÉE OR 4 TO 6
AS AN APPETIZER

2 tablespoons olive oil
4 garlic cloves, chopped
3 chorizo sausages, casings removed and cut into medium dice
2 leeks, well washed and thinly sliced
1 carrot, peeled and cut into medium dice
2 teaspoons curry powder
1 teaspoon ground cumin
1 teaspoon Hungarian paprika
½ teaspoon ground coriander
1½ cups chopped fresh or canned tomatoes
2½ to 3 pounds mussels, scrubbed and debearded
2 cups cooked chick peas, rinsed
1 cup dry white wine

*2 cups Chicken Broth (page 38) or canned low-sodium
     chicken broth*
⅓ cup chopped fresh cilantro leaves, for garnish
⅓ cup chopped scallions, for garnish

Place a large saucepan over medium-high heat and when it is hot, add the oil. Add the garlic and cook until it is golden and lightly toasted, about 2 to 3 minutes. Add the chorizo and cook until the chorizo begins to caramelize, about 2 minutes. Add the leeks, carrot, curry powder, cumin, paprika, and coriander, stirring well after each addition, and cook for 1 minute.

Add the tomatoes, mussels, chick peas, and wine, stirring well after each addition. Cook until the liquid has reduced by one quarter, about 10 minutes. Add the chicken broth, reduce the heat to medium-low, and cook for 20 minutes.

Serve garnished with the cilantro and scallions.

GRILLED MARINATED TUNA

$\mathcal{T}$his is a very flavorful, simple dish. If you put the fish in the marinade in the morning, you'll have a quick weeknight dinner.

SERVES 6

MARINADE:
¼ cup olive oil
2 garlic cloves, finely chopped
2 teaspoons grated orange zest
2 tablespoons grated peeled fresh ginger
½ bunch fresh cilantro, leaves only, chopped

6 6- to 8-ounce very fresh bluefin or yellowfin tuna steaks,
    1½ to 2 inches thick

1 teaspoon kosher salt
½ teaspoon black pepper
Citrus Aïoli (page 36)
6 fresh cilantro sprigs, for garnish

Place the olive oil, garlic, orange zest, ginger, and cilantro in a large glass or ceramic bowl and stir to combine. Add the tuna, cover, and refrigerate for 4 hours, or overnight.

Prepare the grill or preheat the broiler.

Sprinkle the tuna with the salt and pepper, place about 3 to 4 inches from the heat source, and grill or broil for about 5 to 6 minutes per side; the tuna should still be rare.

Drizzle with the aïoli and garnish with the cilantro sprigs.

GRILLED TUNA WITH ZA'ATAR AND FRESH FIG SAUCE

Za'atar is an oregano-based spice mix from the Middle East, the ingredients of which vary from area to area. It's a great combination with the jam-like fig sauce and the rich tuna.

SERVES 4

4 8-ounce very fresh bluefin or yellowfin tuna steaks, 1½ to 2 inches thick
2 tablespoons chopped peeled fresh ginger
¼ cup pomegranate molasses (available at Middle Eastern specialty
    food stores or by mail order)
4 scallions, thinly sliced
2 tablespoons za'atar (available in Middle Eastern specialty food stores
    or by mail order—see page 351)

FIG SAUCE:
2 tablespoons chopped slab bacon or chopped high-quality thick-sliced
    lean bacon
1 teaspoon unsalted butter
¼ chopped Spanish onion
2 cinnamon sticks
½ cup fresh orange juice
4 fresh figs, quartered through the stem end, leaving the root end intact
1 cup Dark Stock (page 40), Chicken Broth (page 38), or canned
    low-sodium chicken broth
2 tablespoons balsamic vinegar
2 tablespoons honey

1 teaspoon kosher salt
½ teaspoon black pepper

To marinate the tuna: Place the ginger, molasses, scallions, and za'atar in a shallow bowl and stir to mix well. Add the tuna and cover with the marinade. Cover and refrigerate for 1 hour.

Prepare the grill.

To make the sauce: Place a large skillet over medium-high heat and when it is hot, add the bacon and butter and cook until the bacon renders its fat. Add the onion, cinnamon sticks, orange juice, figs, stock, vinegar, and honey, stirring well after each addition, and bring to a boil. Cook for 5 minutes.

Sprinkle the tuna with the salt and pepper, place about 3 to 4 inches from the heat source, and grill until the outside is charred and the inside is very rare, about 4 minutes per side.

Spoon the fresh fig sauce over the tuna, and serve immediately.

Char-Grilled Tuna and Avocado Salad with Toasted Corn Vinaigrette

*T*his is a summertime staple in our house. There is no better combination than the freshly caught tuna, sun-warmed avocado, and the peppery extra-virgin olive oil.

■ *I am concerned that the popularity of fresh tuna will lead to the more widespread practice of netting, which scoops up innocent passersby, like dolphin, who get tangled in the nets and drown. Try to buy only line-caught tuna.*

SERVES 6

1¼ pounds very fresh bluefin or yellowfin tuna, cut into 1-inch cubes

MARINADE:
Grated zest of 1 orange
2 tablespoons chopped fresh basil leaves
1 tablespoon chopped fresh rosemary leaves
¼ cup extra-virgin olive oil
2 garlic cloves, chopped
1 teaspoon chopped peeled fresh ginger

TOASTED CORN VINAIGRETTE:
8 tablespoons extra-virgin olive oil
1½ cups fresh corn kernels
1 red onion, finely chopped

4 scallions, chopped
1 tablespoon chopped peeled fresh ginger
2 garlic cloves, chopped
½ cup balsamic vinegar
Juice of 1 orange
2 tablespoons chopped fresh basil leaves
1 tablespoon fresh thyme leaves
1 tablespoon chopped fresh cilantro leaves
1 teaspoon kosher salt
½ teaspoon black pepper

6 cups mixed greens
1½ ripe avocados, peeled, pitted, and sliced
Fresh cilantro sprigs, for garnish

To marinate the tuna: Place the orange zest, basil, rosemary, olive oil, garlic cloves, and ginger in a large glass or ceramic bowl and stir to mix well. Add the tuna and cover with the marinade. Cover and refrigerate for 1 to 2 hours.

To make the corn vinaigrette: Place a large skillet over medium-high heat and when it is hot, add 2 tablespoons of the olive oil. Add the corn and cook until it has browned, about 4 minutes. Add the onion and scallions and cook until they are golden, about 3 to 4 minutes. Add the ginger and garlic and cook for 2 minutes. Off the heat, add the balsamic vinegar, orange juice, the remaining 6 tablespoons olive oil, the basil, thyme, cilantro, salt, and pepper, stirring well after each addition. Let cool to room temperature.

Prepare the grill. Place a piece of mesh over the grill to prevent the tuna from falling through the grates.

Place the tuna on the grill and cook, turning constantly, until the outside is charred and the inside is still rare, about 4 minutes.

Place 1 cup of greens on each plate and top with the avocado. Place the tuna on top of the avocado and drizzle with the corn dressing. Garnish with cilantro sprigs and serve immediately.

■ *GRILL TALK*

Even after eight years of building three different fires every night, I am still fascinated and mesmerized by the fire. The coziness, romance, and passion of the fire directly translate to the food (not to mention the hardwood charcoal and wood bill that exceeds $20,000 annually at Olives alone). And even though there are millions of books on grilling, I want to add my own two cents' worth.

True to the Mediterranean cooking that inspires me, I think it's important to use natural fuel sources, such as hardwood charcoal and wood, which add a smokiness, char, and flavor that cannot be obtained from using a gas grill or charcoal briquettes.

To prepare the grill, use a metal chimney. Fill the upper portion with hardwood charcoal and the bottom portion with two crumpled sheets of newspaper. Place the chimney on top of additional charcoal placed in the bottom of the grill and light the paper. When the charcoal in the chimney is red-hot, after about 20 minutes, dump it into the grill and spread it around evenly. While the coals are burning, brush the grate clean with a wire brush and oil the grate generously. Place the well-oiled grate on the fire to ensure that the grate will be hot and that the food will sear immediately when placed on it. When the coals have burned down to a medium heat, after about 10 minutes, you're ready to cook. The distance between the charcoal and the grate should be no more than 8 inches. If necessary, you can easily achieve this by placing bricks on the bottom of your grill and building the fire on top of them.

How do you know when the food is ready? Don't trust anyone's guidelines. Don't walk away. Don't rely on timers. Stand there and watch. And watch. Only experience will tell you. And err on the side of undercooking. You can always put the food back on the grill.

GRILLED MOLASSES-CURED TUNA

The smoke and molasses flavors intensify the meatiness of the tuna.
Serve with a side dish of plain Corn Cakes (page 68).

SERVES 4

MOLASSES CURE:
2 tablespoons molasses
2 tablespoons honey
1 tablespoon ground ginger
1 tablespoon Hungarian paprika
2 scallions, white and green parts, minced
2 tablespoons chopped fresh cilantro leaves
2 tablespoons olive oil

4 6-ounce very fresh bluefin or yellowfin tuna steaks, about 1½
*   to 2 inches thick*

1 teaspoon kosher salt
½ teaspoon black pepper
1 tablespoon chopped fresh cilantro leaves
1 tablespoon chopped scallions, white and green parts

To make the molasses cure: Place the molasses, honey, ginger, paprika,
scallions, cilantro, and oil in a shallow nonreactive bowl and stir well to mix.
Add the tuna and cover with the marinade. Cover and refrigerate overnight,
turning occasionally.

Prepare the grill or preheat the broiler.

Sprinkle the tuna with the salt and pepper, place about 3 to 4 inches
from the heat source, and cook until medium-rare, about 3 to 4 minutes per
side. Sprinkle with the cilantro and scallions and serve immediately.

BASQUE STEW WITH TUNA

*T*he Basque region of Spain boasts a culture and cuisine that I admire: a little bit radical, offbeat, individualistic, and strong. I learned just how strong-willed and opinionated by dining and cooking in some of San Sebastián's men's clubs, where men gather solely for the purpose of discussing food. The bold Basque flavors work well with the meaty tuna.

Serve with bread and a green salad and a dry, crisp Sauvignon or Fumé Blanc.

SERVES 6 TO 8

1 pound slab or high-quality thick-sliced lean bacon, cubed
3 anchovy fillets, chopped
2 Spanish onions, chopped
2 carrots, peeled and cut into medium dice
3 to 4 garlic cloves, chopped
3 Idaho potatoes, cut into large dice
½ head Savoy cabbage, cut into large dice
8 roasted plum tomatoes (page 31), quartered
3 roasted red peppers (page 48), cut into large dice
2 cups dry white wine
Zest of 1 lemon, cut into strips
½ cup fresh basil leaves, torn, plus 1 tablespoon chopped leaves
½ fennel bulb, trimmed, cored, and sliced
2 teaspoons kosher salt
1 teaspoon black pepper
2 pounds very fresh bluefin or yellowfin tuna, cut into 1½-inch cubes
1 tablespoon Dijon mustard
1 tablespoon chopped fresh cilantro leaves
1 tablespoon olive oil

Place a large deep skillet over medium-high heat and when it is hot, add the bacon. When the fat begins to render, add the anchovy fillets, onions, carrots, garlic, potatoes, Savoy cabbage, tomatoes, and peppers, stirring well after each addition, and cook for 10 minutes. Add the wine, lemon zest, the torn basil, the fennel, 1 teaspoon of the salt, and ½ teaspoon of the pepper. Reduce the heat to low and cook, uncovered, for 2 hours.

Just prior to serving, combine the tuna, mustard, chopped basil, cilantro, and the remaining 1 teaspoon salt and ½ teaspoon pepper in a bowl. Place a skillet over medium-high heat and when it is hot, add the oil. Add the tuna and cook until it is browned on all sides but still rare in the middle, about 3 to 4 minutes. (It is very important that the tuna be rare, or it will overcook in the hot stew and be dry and tough.)

Add the tuna to the stew and stir gently until all the ingredients are well combined. Serve at once.

SOFT-SHELL CRAB SANDWICH WITH SPICY AÏOLI

*T*he Cadillac of American peasant cooking, soft-shell crabs are probably the most luxurious soul food I know of. Over the years I've made hundreds and hundreds of crab dishes and, by far, the soft-shell crab stands out as my favorite crab. As exotic as the preparations may get, there's still no better way of eating a soft-shell crab than between two slices of bread.

■ *CRAB TALK*

Soft-shell crabs are blue crabs from the Chesapeake Bay and are available from late May to late August. Harvesting them presents a challenge because the process of the crabs shedding their hard shells and beginning to grow new tough hard shells takes place over only a few hours. They must be watched carefully and removed as soon as they shed their shells. They must be packed and shipped immediately, and they live only a few days out of water. You can find them frozen all year round, but I don't recommend using the frozen crabs.

SERVES 4

¼ *cup light or heavy cream*
¼ *cup semolina*
¼ *cup finely grated Parmesan cheese*
2 *tablespoons all-purpose flour*
2 *tablespoons olive oil*
12 *soft-shell crabs, cleaned (see next page)*
8 *slices Tuscan bread or other country bread*

1 large Spanish onion, thinly sliced
4 thin slices smoked ham (about 4 to 6 ounces)
½ head Boston lettuce, well washed, dried, and torn
2 tablespoons Spicy Aïoli (see page 35)

Pour the cream into a shallow bowl. Combine the semolina, Parmesan, and flour in another shallow bowl.

Place a large skillet over a medium-high heat and when it is hot, add the oil. Dip the crabs in the cream and then in the semolina mixture. Place in the skillet and cook until browned, about 2 to 3 minutes per side. Place 3 crabs each on 4 slices of the bread. Add the onions and ham to the skillet. Cook until the onions are lightly browned but still somewhat crunchy, about 3 minutes. Place the onions, ham, and lettuce on top of the crabs and drizzle with the aïoli. Put the remaining bread on top, press down firmly, and serve immediately.

■ *CLEANING SOFT-SHELL CRABS*

Be sure to buy crabs that are live and kicking. Turn each crab on its back so that the legs come up and grab your wrist. With a knife or scissors, cut the head off just below the feelers, and squeeze out the green glop. Flip the crab back over and underneath the soft green shell you will see gills, which look like little plastic tubes. Take the edge of the knife and scrape from the center out. (Be sure to take the gills out, as they can be very bitter.) Pull the tail flap out and cut at the base. Cover the crabs with milk and soak for about 15 minutes.

PARMESAN-CRUSTED SOFT-SHELL CRABS WITH SUCCOTASH VINAIGRETTE

*O*ne of the most appealing things about living in New England is having four very distinctive seasons. This dish exemplifies the summer: the early harvest corn from the north, the local fava beans, and the soft-shell crabs from the Chesapeake. I can't wait for soft-shell season, and then when it ends, truth be told, I'm glad to see them go, because by then I've just about exhausted the possibilities—and my taste buds.

■ *In addition to adding great flavor to the soft-shell crabs, the combination of corn and lima beans makes another complete protein.*

SERVES 4

SUCCOTASH VINAIGRETTE:
1 cup thin strips slab bacon or thin strips high-quality thick-sliced
*   lean bacon*
1 tablespoon minced garlic
½ cup fresh corn kernels
½ cup fresh fava beans or fresh or frozen lima beans
1 tablespoon balsamic vinegar
1 teaspoon fresh lemon juice (about ¼ lemon)
¼ cup chopped scallions, white and green parts
1 tablespoon chopped fresh basil leaves
⅛ teaspoon kosher salt
⅛ teaspoon black pepper

⅔ cup buttermilk
¼ cup all-purpose flour
¼ cup semolina
¼ cup finely grated Parmesan cheese
¼ teaspoon kosher salt
¼ teaspoon black pepper
12 soft-shell crabs, cleaned (see page 299)
2 tablespoons olive oil

SAUTÉED PEA SHOOTS:
1 tablespoon olive oil
1 tablespoon minced peeled fresh ginger
6 ounces pea shoots
¼ teaspoon kosher salt
⅛ teaspoon black pepper

To make the succotash vinaigrette: Place a large skillet over medium-high heat and when it is hot, add the bacon and cook until it has rendered its fat, about 6 to 8 minutes. Discard the fat. Add the garlic, corn, and beans and cook for 3 minutes. Add the balsamic vinegar, lemon juice, scallions, basil, salt, and pepper. Set aside.

To cook the crabs: Place the buttermilk in a shallow bowl. Combine the flour, semolina, Parmesan, salt, and pepper in another bowl. Dip the crabs in the buttermilk and then in the flour mixture.

Place a large skillet over medium-high heat and when it is hot, add the oil. Add the crabs, one at a time, making sure that the pan is hot before each addition, and cook for about 2 to 3 minutes per side. You may have to cook the crabs in batches. Transfer to a plate.

To cook the pea shoots: Reheat the pan and add the oil. Add the ginger and cook for 2 minutes. Add the pea shoots, salt, and pepper and cook until the pea shoots begin to wilt, about 2 minutes.

Place the pea shoots on the plate. Top with the crabs and then the vinaigrette.

NOTE: *Pea shoots are available at Chinese markets. If you can't find them, substitute snow peas or sugar snaps and increase the cooking time to 4 minutes.*

PAN-FRIED TROUT WITH CRAB AND AMANDINE VINAIGRETTE

*A*lthough I think Trout Amandine is pretty boring, it *is* one of the great classic dishes that have inspired many other great dishes by a multitude of chefs. When I worked at La Côte Basque in New York City, we made just about every variation you could imagine, among them Dover Sole Amandine and Coquille St.-Jacques Amandine. Here I've added crab to create a more elegant dish, a harbinger of the light dishes of the summer.

You can substitute eel, black bass, or swordfish for the trout.

> ■ *There is a little village called Scheggina in the Umbrian region of Italy that seems to have been untouched by time. It is an area surrounded by mountain streams filled with trout and land filled with black truffles. I went there to visit the Urbani truffle-processing plant and had dinner in a little no-name-hotel dining room. The first course was a memorable truffle crostini: grilled sliced bread slathered with a thick puree of black truffles. Next came tagliatelle with a thick puree of black truffles. Finally, the trout, boned and stuffed with, yes, you got it, a thick puree of black truffles. A bottle of local red wine and, oh, we were in heaven. I'm not sure I've ever tasted a fish so incredible.*

SERVES 4

1 cup buttermilk
¼ cup Dijon mustard
4 10-ounce trout, butterflied and boned by your fishmonger

AMANDINE VINAIGRETTE:
⅓ to ½ pound asparagus, woody ends trimmed,
 chopped
¼ cup coarsely chopped slab bacon or coarsely chopped
 high-quality thick-sliced lean bacon
½ cup almonds, coarsely chopped
2 beefsteak tomatoes, diced
2 tablespoons chopped fresh flat-leaf parsley leaves
2 to 3 tablespoons fresh lemon juice
 (to taste)
1 teaspoon Dijon mustard
1 tablespoon buttermilk
½ pound fresh crabmeat, picked over
½ teaspoon kosher salt
¼ teaspoon black pepper

¼ cup all-purpose flour
½ teaspoon kosher salt
¼ teaspoon black pepper
1 tablespoon olive oil

Place the buttermilk and mustard in a large glass or ceramic bowl and add the trout. Cover and refrigerate for 20 minutes to 2 hours.

To make the vinaigrette: Place the asparagus in a small bowl and cover with boiling water. Let sit for 2 minutes, drain, rinse with cold water, and place in a mixing bowl. Set aside.

Place a small skillet over medium-high heat and when it is hot, add the bacon. Cook until the bacon has rendered its fat. Add the bacon to the reserved asparagus and discard the bacon fat.

Reheat the pan, add the almonds, and cook, shaking the pan occasionally, until they are toasted, about 2 to 3 minutes. Add the almonds to the reserved asparagus. Add the tomatoes, parsley, lemon juice, mustard, buttermilk, crabmeat, salt, and pepper and toss very gently.

Place the flour on a plate. Remove the trout from the buttermilk, season with the salt and pepper, and then dip in the flour.

Place a large skillet over medium-high heat and when it is hot, add the oil. Place the trout in the pan and cook until it is browned and slightly crispy, about 2 minutes per side. Transfer to 4 plates and served topped with the vinaigrette.

SWORDFISH WITH CLAMS, CILANTRO, AND CORN BROTH

*S*wordfish is one of my favorite fish for grilling. Unfortunately, it's hard to get great quality and as the world's supply becomes more and more depleted, I try not to overuse it (it's my own little conservation plan). The freshest I've ever found is at Poole's Fish Market in Menemsha, the small fishing village on Martha's Vineyard where *Jaws* was filmed. Sweet, firm, meaty, and aromatic, this is a great late-summer dish that's perfect to prepare when the corn has just been harvested.

SERVES 8

½ cup chopped slab bacon or chopped high-quality thick-sliced lean bacon
1 bunch scallions, white and green parts, chopped
1 small bunch fresh thyme, chopped (leaves only)
2 strips lemon zest
6 garlic cloves, peeled
2 tablespoons olive oil
8 8-ounce swordfish steaks, about 1½ to 2 inches thick
1 teaspoon kosher salt
½ teaspoon black pepper

BROTH:
¼ cup extra-virgin olive oil
2 shallots, coarsely chopped
2 cups fresh corn kernels
32 littleneck clams
4 cups Corn Stock (page 44) or Chicken Broth (page 38)
¼ cup chopped scallions
¼ cup chopped fresh cilantro leaves

Place the bacon in a food processor fitted with a steel blade. Add the scallions, thyme, lemon zest, and garlic and the 2 tablespoons oil and pulse until the mixture forms a chunky paste.

Lather the paste on both sides of the swordfish and place the swordfish on a plate. Cover and refrigerate for 1 hour.

Prepare the grill.

Sprinkle the swordfish with the salt and pepper and place on the grill, 3 to 4 inches from the heat source. Grill for about 5 minutes per side, being careful not to overcook. Set the swordfish aside, covered loosely.

To make the broth: Place a large skillet over medium-high heat and when it is hot, add the extra-virgin olive oil. Add the shallots and cook for 2 minutes. Add the corn and cook until the kernels are toasted, about 4 minutes. Add the littlenecks and the corn stock and simmer until the clams open, about 5 minutes. Discard any clams that do not open.

Place the swordfish in four shallow bowls and surround with the broth. Garnish with the scallions and cilantro and serve immediately.

POACHED SKATE IN PORCINI BROTH

I designed this dish to be low in fat, but I didn't want to sacrifice flavor. The rich broth of the porcini mushrooms is a perfect vehicle for the briny taste of the clams and the rich, meaty texture of the skate wings.

Serve with Shaved Raw Fennel and Red Onion Salad (page 121) or steamed potatoes.

■ *Skate, which some compare to scallops in taste, is usually sold as wings rather than the whole fish. It has a very, very, very short shelf life, so be sure to buy it on the day you want to use it. If the flesh is dull or off-color, don't buy it: it should be a vibrant white with a reddish tint.*

SERVES 4

1 teaspoon olive oil
2 tablespoons finely chopped smoked turkey
1 garlic clove, minced
1 tablespoon chopped fresh rosemary leaves or 1 teaspoon dried rosemary
2 carrots, peeled and minced
1 celery stalk, minced
1 shallot, minced
1 scallion (white part only), minced
3 roasted Vidalia onions (see page 30), thinly sliced
6 ounces fresh porcini mushrooms, thinly sliced (about 1 cup),
    or dried porcini
1 teaspoon kosher salt
½ teaspoon black pepper

1½ to 1¾ cups Chicken Broth (see page 38) or canned low-sodium
    chicken broth
½ cup dry white wine
1 pound boneless skate wings, skinned
20 littleneck clams, scrubbed
2 tablespoons chopped fresh flat-leaf parsley leaves

Place a large skillet over medium heat and when it is hot, add the oil. Add the turkey and cook for 2 minutes. Add the garlic, rosemary, carrots, celery, shallot, scallion, roasted onions, mushrooms, ½ teaspoon of the salt, and ¼ teaspoon of the pepper, stirring well after each addition, and cook until the vegetables are just beginning to get crisp, about 3 to 5 minutes.

Add the chicken broth and wine and bring to a boil. Reduce the heat to low and simmer for 10 minutes. Sprinkle the skate with the remaining ½ teaspoon salt and ¼ teaspoon pepper, gently lower into the broth, and cook about 2 minutes. Carefully transfer the skate to four shallow bowls and set aside.

Increase the heat to medium-high and bring the broth to a boil. Cook until it has reduced by one half, about 5 minutes. Add the clams and cook until they open, about 7 minutes. Discard any clams that do not open.

Surround the skate with the broth and clams, sprinkle with the parsley, and serve immediately.

BARBECUED SHRIMP WITH CHORIZO SAUCE

I'm a big fan of shrimp, and all members of the shrimp family, but not unless it really comes right out of the water. The best is Gulf shrimp, but you can also use fresh Maine shrimp or prawns that are now being harvested out of Texas, Santa Barbara, California, Alaska, and Hawaii. The meat should be firm and sweet, never mushy.

This may seem like an outrageous and uncommon treatment for shrimp but it's one of the greatest: the combination of the smoky, spicy chorizo and the sweet and succulent meat of the shrimp is a classic. The chorizo sauce is also good on barbecued chicken.

Serve with a simple steamed rice or, if you're going to indulge, you might as well have the Garlic Mashed Potatoes (page 175).

■ *If fresh shrimp is unavailable, you can buy Ocean Garden, a high-quality frozen shrimp. It comes out of the Gulf of Mexico and from along the Eastern seaboard. It is usually pink and white, and has a firm texture and the truest shrimp flavor. These typically cost more than other frozen shrimp but are well worth it.*

SERVES 4 TO 6

30 large shrimp in the shell, butterflied and deveined
2 tablespoons olive oil
¼ teaspoon minced Scotch bonnet or jalapeño pepper
1 teaspoon minced peeled fresh ginger
1 garlic clove, minced

CHORIZO SAUCE:

1 tablespoon olive oil

2 chorizo sausages, cut into small dice

½ cup finely chopped fresh or canned tomatoes

¼ cup minced peeled fresh ginger

2 garlic cloves, thinly sliced

2 shallots, thinly sliced

½ Scotch bonnet or jalapeño pepper, seeded and minced

1 cup balsamic vinegar

½ cup soy sauce

¼ cup honey

1 tablespoon lightly packed brown sugar

1 tablespoon Worcestershire sauce

½ cup water

2 tablespoons unsalted butter, at room temperature

2 tablespoons chopped fresh cilantro leaves, for garnish

2 tablespoons chopped scallions, white and green parts, for garnish

Place the shrimp, 2 tablespoons oil, chile peppers, ginger, and garlic in a large glass or ceramic bowl, cover, and refrigerate overnight.

To make the chorizo sauce: Place a large skillet over medium-high heat and when it is hot, add the 1 tablespoon oil. Add the chorizo and tomatoes and cook until the chorizo has caramelized, about 5 minutes. Add the ginger, garlic, shallots, and chile peppers, stirring well after each addition, and cook until soft, about 10 minutes.

Add the balsamic vinegar, soy sauce, honey, brown sugar, Worcester-shire, and water, stirring well after each addition, and cook until the sauce is syrupy and thick, about 10 minutes. Place the sauce in a blender and blend until smooth. Add the butter.

Reheat the skillet and when it is hot, add the shrimp, cut side down, and the marinade. Cook until it is pink and opaque throughout, about 2 to 3 minutes. Add the shrimp to the sauce and garnish with the cilantro and scallions.

Roasted Clams with Chicken, Tomatoes, Artichokes, and Bacon

When I was cooking on Martha's Vineyard, I used to wait by the ocean with a bottle of Tabasco in my hand and a shucker in my pocket. As soon as I dug a clam out of the sand, into my mouth it went, spiked with the Tabasco. I swear I used to get my quota just standing there. (I hope there are no game wardens reading this!) In the rare occasions that any made it home, I roasted them.

Serve with roasted new potatoes or Saffron Risotto (page 190).

■ *When buying clams, buy only those that are closed. Discard any that are open or have broken or cracked shells. Just prior to cooking, soak them in cold water to rid them of their salt and grit. Any clams that rise to the surface should be discarded. Scrub the clams well under cold running water.*

SERVES 6

6 chicken thighs
½ teaspoon kosher salt
¼ teaspoon black pepper
¼ cup chopped slab bacon or chopped high-quality thick-sliced lean bacon
3 garlic cloves, thinly sliced
8 to 12 fresh, frozen, or canned artichoke bottoms, thickly sliced
    (see instructions on page 67 for fresh)
24 clams, scrubbed
2 large fresh yellow or red tomatoes, chopped
1 heaping tablespoon chopped fresh thyme leaves

Preheat the oven to 425 degrees.

Sprinkle the chicken thighs with the salt and pepper.

Place a large, ovenproof skillet over medium-high heat and when it is hot, add the bacon. When it begins to render its fat, add the garlic and chicken thighs and cook until the thighs are browned, about 3 minutes on each side. Add the artichoke bottoms, clams, and tomatoes, stirring well after each addition, and cook for 5 minutes. Sprinkle with the thyme.

Place the pan in the oven and roast until the clams open and the chicken is cooked, about 20 minutes. Discard any clams that do not open, and serve in shallow bowls.

■ *S T R I P E D B A S S T A L K*

I love almost every kind of fish, but hands down, striped bass is my favorite fish that swims the ocean. My idea of pure paradise is to catch it early in the morning off Nantucket or Martha's Vineyard and barbecue it with friends the same evening while gazing at the sunset over the ocean. Pairing the succulent, opaque white, meaty, luscious, and sweet bass with freshly dug new potatoes, local corn grilled in its husk, and a spicy salad of native greens is a celebration of the summer harvest, and absolute ecstasy. Please pass the Chardonnay.

BAKED WHOLE BASS WITH APPLE AND FENNEL

I don't often mix fruit and fish, but this dish is an exception. The fennel helps cut the sweetness of the apples. Apples and fennel are a perfect fall combination.

SERVES 6

1½ fennel bulbs, trimmed, cored, and thinly sliced
½ Spanish onion, thinly sliced
½ cup diced slab bacon or diced high-quality thick-sliced lean bacon
1 tablespoon olive oil
1 2-pound bass, skin scored
1 teaspoon kosher salt
½ teaspoon black pepper
4 bay leaves
1¾ cups apple cider
2 Cortland or McIntosh apples, cored and thinly sliced (peeled if desired)
20 to 24 clams, scrubbed
Greens from 1 bunch scallions
1 small bunch fresh thyme

Preheat the oven to 350 degrees.

Cover the bottom of an 8 x 12-inch baking pan with the fennel and then layer with the onion. Sprinkle with the bacon and drizzle with the olive oil. Lay the bass on top, and sprinkle with the salt, pepper, and bay leaves.

Surround the bass with the apple cider, apple slices, and clams. Scatter the scallion greens and thyme over the top. Place in the oven and cook until the clams open and the fish is cooked, about 30 minutes. Discard any clams that do not open.

Remove the bay leaves and serve the fish on a large platter.

ARTICHOKE-CRUSTED SALMON WITH MINT VINAIGRETTE

I have a love-hate relationship with salmon. I have some friends who regularly go fishing for wild salmon in British Columbia. When they return, we marinate and grill it. Served with a Pouilly Fumé, it makes me swoon. On the other hand, I've gone to restaurants and eaten salmon so old and so overcooked I couldn't even think about eating the ecstatically good wild salmon for months.

At first glance, this combination of flavors might seem bizarre, but they create an elegant, delicious, and complex dish that is incredibly easy to make. In addition, it's very low in fat.

■ *Once caught only seasonally, salmon is now farm-raised in the Pacific Northwest, Canada, Norway, and Chile and available all year round. It lacks the flavor of the wild salmon, but at Olives we use the flavorful, fat-marbled Atlantic Coast variety, which arrives within twenty-four hours of being harvested. Use it immediately, because it spoils very quickly.*

SERVES 4

ARTICHOKE CRUST:
*6 fresh, frozen, or canned artichoke bottoms (see instructions on
    page 67 for fresh)*
3 garlic cloves
¼ cup buttermilk or yogurt
1 tablespoon Dijon mustard
2 tablespoons plain dry bread crumbs
1 teaspoon fresh thyme leaves or ⅓ teaspoon dried thyme
½ teaspoon kosher salt
¼ teaspoon black pepper

MINT VINAIGRETTE:
1 beefsteak tomato, minced
2 shallots, minced
2 tablespoons chopped fresh mint leaves
2 tablespoons fresh lemon juice
1 teaspoon sherry vinegar
½ teaspoon kosher salt
¼ teaspoon black pepper

4 6-ounce salmon fillets
½ teaspoon kosher salt
¼ teaspoon black pepper
12 baby artichokes, cooked, thinly sliced through the heart (optional), or
    2 tablespoons bread crumbs

Preheat the oven to 350 degrees.

To make the artichoke crust: Place the artichoke bottoms, garlic, buttermilk, mustard, bread crumbs, thyme, salt, and pepper in a food processor fitted with a steel blade and process until smooth.

To make the mint vinaigrette: Combine the tomato, shallots, mint, lemon juice, vinegar, salt, and pepper in a small bowl. Set aside.

Sprinkle the salmon with the salt and pepper. Divide the artichoke crust into 4 portions and place it on the top of the salmon fillets, patting it down to form a crust. Cover the artichoke crust with the artichoke slices or sprinkle with bread crumbs.

Place a large ovenproof nonstick skillet over medium-high heat and when it is hot, add the salmon fillets, skin side down. Cook until the skin is crispy, about 2 minutes. Transfer to the oven and bake until the salmon is just rare, about 10 minutes.

Drizzle with the mint vinaigrette and serve immediately.

ALMOND-CRUSTED SNAPPER

*H*ere's another way to use the classic amandine flavors. I love the combination of the rich nuts and sharp mustard with the meaty, firm texture and sweet, strong flavor of the snapper. Serve with Saffron Risotto (page 190) and Shaved Raw Fennel and Red Onion Salad (page 121).

SERVES 4

½ cup shelled almonds
1 bulb roasted garlic (see page 28), peeled
2 tablespoons Dijon mustard
2 tablespoons virgin olive oil
1 tablespoon chopped fresh flat-leaf parsley leaves
1 teaspoon chopped fresh rosemary leaves or ⅓ teaspoon dried rosemary
1 teaspoon kosher salt
½ teaspoon black pepper
1 tablespoon olive oil
4 6-ounce red snapper fillets, preferably Gulf Coast, scored on the skin side

Preheat the oven to 400 degrees.

Place the nuts in a large skillet over medium heat and cook, shaking or stirring occasionally, until the nuts are brown, about 3 to 5 minutes. Place in a food processor and pulse until ground.

Place the almonds, roasted garlic, mustard, virgin olive oil, parsley, rosemary, ½ teaspoon of the salt, and ¼ teaspoon of the pepper in a bowl and mash to a paste.

Place a large cast-iron skillet or other heavy ovenproof skillet over medium-high heat and when it is hot, add the olive oil. Sprinkle the snapper with the remaining ½ teaspoon salt and ¼ teaspoon pepper. Add to the pan, skin side down, and cook until skin is crisp, about 2 minutes.

Turn the fillets over and spread the top with the almond mixture. Place in the oven and bake until the crust is well browned, about 6 minutes.

Serve on a large platter.

PAN-GRILLED SQUID
WITH CITRUS AÏOLI

*W*hen squid was just called squid, it was not a popular dish. When it began to be identified as *calamari* (the Italian word for squid) it became exotic and very popular. The cooking method that most people use is deep frying, but my favorite way is to pan-grill it. (You can also use a wood grill for this recipe.) Serve with a lightly dressed green salad and crusty bread.

SERVES 3 TO 4

■ *On the ferry going to Nantucket Island, I read a brochure that said that most of the fishing trawlers I saw were fishing for squid that was on its way to Europe—and the freezer.*

One of the best and most simple preparations for squid is to toss it with olive oil, salt, and pepper and grill it. When you take it off the grill, drizzle it with a little extra virgin olive oil and lemon juice.

1 pound squid bodies, cleaned and cut into thin rings
1 teaspoon kosher salt
1 teaspoon black pepper
1 tablespoon olive oil
2 to 3 garlic cloves, minced
1 leek, well washed and thinly sliced
½ small chorizo sausage, diced (optional)
2 carrots, peeled and cut into small dice
2 celery stalks, cut into small dice
2 cups dry red wine
2 tablespoons balsamic vinegar

2 tablespoons unsalted butter, at room temperature
½ cup chopped scallions
Citrus Aïoli (page 36)

Sprinkle the squid with the salt and pepper. Place a large cast-iron skillet over medium-high heat and when it is hot, add the squid. Cook for about 3 minutes, or until browned. Stir well and remove the squid.

Reheat the pan and add the oil. Add the garlic, leek, chorizo, if desired, carrots, and celery, stirring well after each addition, and cook until the vegetables have caramelized, about 8 minutes.

Add the wine and vinegar and cook until the liquid has reduced by half, about 7 minutes. Add the butter, scallions and the reserved squid, stirring well after each addition, and cook until the squid is hot, about 1 minute. Transfer to a platter and drizzle with the aïoli.

BLACK SEA BASS WITH GREEN OLIVE SAUCE

*J*ust before we opened Olives, Olivia and I went to Viareggio, Italy, to buy restaurant equipment. When lunchtime came, the owners of the shop we were visiting graciously offered to take us to their local seafood joint. We started with the usual array of antipasto, followed by a great spaghetti dish, and then finished with the most incredible entrée, Roasted Bass with Green Olive Sauce. When I returned to Olives I tried to replicate the dish. I'm a lousy copycat, and this is what I came up with (actually not a bad interpretation).

You can substitute striped bass or halibut for the black sea bass.

SERVES 4

GREEN OLIVE SAUCE:
1 tablespoon olive oil
1 garlic clove, finely chopped
2 shallots, finely diced
2 cups dry white wine
4 anchovy fillets, minced
2 to 3 tablespoons green olive puree (available at specialty food stores)
2 cups Chicken Broth (page 38), canned low-sodium chicken broth,
    or water
2 tablespoons unsalted butter, at room temperature

4 8- to 10-ounce black sea bass fillets
1 teaspoon kosher salt
½ teaspoon black pepper
1 tablespoon olive oil
12 green olives, pitted and coarsely chopped, for garnish

To make the green olive sauce: Place a large saucepan over medium heat and when it is hot, add the 1 tablespoon olive oil. Add the garlic and shallots and cook until they are translucent, about 3 to 4 minutes. Add the white wine and cook until it has reduced to about ¼ cup, about 20 minutes.

Add the anchovy fillets, green olive puree, and chicken broth and cook until the sauce has reduced to about 1½ cups. Remove the pan from the heat and whisk in the butter. Cover to keep warm.

Sprinkle the bass with the salt and pepper.

Place a large cast-iron pan over medium-high heat and when it is hot, add the tablespoon of oil. Add the bass, skin side down, and cook until lightly browned, about 3 to 4 minutes per side.

Place the fillets on a plate, top with the green olive sauce, and garnish with the chopped green olives.

STEAMED TAGINE OF HALIBUT WITH MOROCCAN-SPICED SPAGHETTI SQUASH

I doubt that spaghetti squash is available in Morocco. However, I've taken some classic Moroccan spices and combined them in a way that makes the bland squash more interesting.

I was recently at a conference in Morocco where we debated the preservation of traditional Moroccan cooking versus the modern adaptation. I believe that both are valid and that as long as one is a student first and an interpreter second, it is impossible to bastardize Moroccan or any other established traditional cuisine. You must respect it but not hesitate to have fun with it. Never forget that the most important quality of food is that it taste good.

SERVES 4

2 medium-size spaghetti squash, halved

YOGURT SAUCE:
¾ cup plain low-fat yogurt
2 teaspoons chopped fresh flat-leaf parsley flakes
3 scallion greens, chopped
¼ teaspoon toasted sesame oil
¼ teaspoon kosher salt
¼ teaspoon black pepper

1 tablespoon olive oil
3 garlic cloves, thinly sliced
1½ teaspoons curry powder
½ head Savoy cabbage, thinly sliced

1 cup Chicken Broth (page 38) or canned low-sodium chicken broth
3 beefsteak tomatoes or 8 to 10 canned plum tomatoes, cut into small dice
4 6-ounce halibut fillets
1 teaspoon kosher salt
½ teaspoon black pepper

Preheat the oven to 425 degrees.

Place the squash, cut side down, in a large roasting pan and add 1 inch of water. Place in the oven and bake for about 1¼ hours, or until the squash is very soft. When it is cool enough to handle, discard the seeds and scoop out the flesh. Set aside.

To make the yogurt sauce: Combine the yogurt, parsley, scallion greens, sesame oil, salt, and pepper in a small bowl. Cover and refrigerate.

Place a large skillet over medium-high heat and when it is hot, add the olive oil. Add the garlic, curry powder, cabbage, broth, tomatoes, and reserved squash, stirring well after each addition, and cook for 5 minutes.

Sprinkle the halibut with salt and pepper and lay it on top of the squash mixture and cook until the halibut is opaque throughout, about 5 minutes.

Serve with a generous dollop of yogurt sauce on top of each fillet.

PAELLA

Whenever I'm in a Spanish restaurant, whether here or in Spain, I always order paella, because I am fascinated by its composition. It should be an exquisite dish but, quite frankly, I have never had one I really liked in a restaurant.

My interpretation uses arborio rice. The stock is redolent of the sea and reflects the natural sweetness of the rice, which blends with the buttery saffron. The seafood must not be overcooked.

I could eat this all the time, and although this recipe uses a large number of ingredients, once you get comfortable with the technique, you can get very creative. As many times as we have made Paella at Olives, it has never come out the same way twice, which is part of its beauty.

SERVES 4

4 chicken thighs
1 large chorizo sausage, sliced
1 tablespoon olive oil
¼ cup thinly sliced garlic
1 Spanish onion, thinly sliced
2 teaspoons kosher salt
1½ teaspoons black pepper
½ to 1 teaspoon crushed red pepper flakes
A large pinch of saffron threads
2 leeks, well washed and chopped
2 cups arborio rice
1 cup canned chopped tomatoes, partially drained
1 cup dry white wine
3 to 3½ cups Lobster Stock (page 42)
8 clams, scrubbed

3 to 3½ cups Chicken Broth (page 38) or canned low-sodium chicken broth
4 ounces oily fish fillets, such as bluefish or mackerel
4 ounces dry white fish fillets, such as cod or monkfish
1 2-pound lobster, cut into eighths (see next page)
8 mussels, scrubbed and debearded
1 cup fresh or frozen green peas
1 cup chopped scallions, for garnish
12 sprigs fresh cilantro, for garnish

Place a large skillet over medium-high heat and when it is hot, add the chicken, skin side down. Cook until the skin is well browned, about 3 to 5 minutes. Turn the chicken over and add the chorizo, and cook until both are well browned and crispy, about 5 minutes; add the oil if the chicken is sticking or the pan seems dry. Add the garlic, onion, 1 teaspoon of the salt, ½ teaspoon of the black pepper, and the red pepper flakes, saffron, and leeks, stirring well after each addition. Cook for 3 minutes. Remove the chicken thighs and set them aside.

Add the rice, tomatoes, and wine and 1 cup of the lobster stock and cook, stirring constantly, until the liquid has been absorbed by the rice. Add the remaining lobster stock, 1 cup at a time, stirring well after each addition, until it has been absorbed by the rice. Add the clams, the reserved chicken thighs, 1 cup of the chicken broth, and the remaining 1 teaspoon salt and 1 teaspoon pepper and cook, stirring, until the chicken broth has been absorbed by the rice. Add the fish, lobster, and mussels and the remaining 2 to 2½ cups of the chicken broth, 1 cup at a time, as needed, and cook, stirring, until it has been absorbed by the rice.

Add the peas and cook until heated through, about 1 minute for fresh and 2 minutes for frozen. Garnish with the scallions and cilantro sprigs, and serve immediately.

■ *LOBSTER TALK*

To cut up a live lobster: Place the lobster on its back, head facing toward you, on a large cutting board and place the tip of a sharp knife or cleaver in the center of the lobster, being sure that the claws are not in the path of the knife. Cut through the head just between the eyes. Turn the lobster around and repeat this same motion, splitting the tail. Remove and discard the body (or save it for stock), head sac, intestine, and tomalley and if it is a female, the roe. To crack the claws, use the back of the knife or cleaver and tap the shell until it cracks. Break off the arms and the claws. Crack the claws in the center.

DESSERTS ■

FALLING CHOCOLATE CAKE
WITH RASPBERRY SAUCE

Debbie Merriam, Olives' first baker, and I came up with this one together. It's never, ever been off the menu, and it never will be.

SERVES 6

RASPBERRY SAUCE:
4 cups fresh or frozen raspberries
½ cup white sugar

CHOCOLATE CAKE:
2 tablespoons unsalted butter, for preparing ramekins
2 tablespoons all-purpose flour, for preparing ramekins
12 ounces bittersweet chocolate, coarsely chopped
1 cup (2 sticks) unsalted butter
1 cup white sugar
½ cup all-purpose flour
6 large eggs

4 cups vanilla ice cream, for serving
2 tablespoons powdered sugar, for garnish
6 fresh mint sprigs, for garnish

To make the raspberry sauce: Place the raspberries and sugar in a small saucepan and bring to a boil, stirring, over high heat. Boil until the sugar dissolves. Let cool.

Place half the sauce in a food processor fitted with a steel blade and puree. Combine with the remaining sauce, cover, and refrigerate until cold.

Preheat the oven to 350 degrees. Generously butter and flour six 8-ounce ramekins.

Place the chocolate and butter in the top of a double boiler over simmering water. Stir until completely melted. Set aside to cool.

Place the sugar, flour, and eggs in a large bowl and beat until thick and fluffy, about 5 minutes. Gently beat in the cooled chocolate mixture.

Pour the batter into the prepared ramekins, filling them two-thirds to three-quarters of the way up the sides. Bake until they begin to puff up, about 15 minutes. Run a knife around the edge of each ramekin and turn the ramekin upside down on a plate to unmold.

Serve each warm cake surrounded by sauce, with a scoop of vanilla ice cream alongside. Garnish with the powdered sugar and sprigs of fresh mint.

GINGERSNAP RISOTTO PUDDING WITH BRANDIED PLUM COMPOTE

*I*f you don't want to make the Brandied Plum Compote, serve this with fresh blueberries.

SERVES 6 TO 8

BRANDIED PLUM COMPOTE:
6 to 8 plums (depending on size), pitted and chopped
½ cup lightly packed dark brown sugar
Grated zest of 1 orange
Juice of 2 oranges
2 bay leaves
1 cup brandy

4 cups water
½ cup roughly chopped fresh ginger
1 vanilla bean, split
2 tablespoons unsalted butter
2 cups arborio rice
½ cup white sugar
Grated zest of 1 orange
2 cups milk
2 cups light or heavy cream
2 large egg yolks
1 cup crumbled high-quality store-bought gingersnaps
¼ cup candied ginger, finely chopped

To make the compote: Place the plums, brown sugar, orange zest and juice, bay leaves, and brandy in a saucepan and bring to a boil over high heat.

Set aside. Reduce the heat to low and cook until the plums are very soft, about 10 to 15 minutes. Set aside.

Place the water, ginger, and vanilla bean in a small saucepan and bring to a boil over medium-high heat. Reduce the heat to low and cook for 10 to 15 minutes. Strain the water and discard the ginger and vanilla bean.

Melt the butter in a large straight-sided nonreactive saucepan over medium heat. Add the rice and stir until it is well coated.

Add 1 cup of the ginger water, the sugar, and the orange zest and cook, stirring constantly, until the liquid is absorbed by the rice. Continue adding the ginger water, 1 cup at a time, stirring until it has been absorbed by the rice. Add the milk, 1 cup at a time, and cook, stirring constantly, until it has been absorbed. Add the cream, 1 cup at a time, and cook, stirring constantly, until the cream has been absorbed, about 18 to 20 minutes.

Off the heat, add the egg yolks very quickly, being careful to stir constantly so they don't curdle. Mix in the gingersnaps and the candied ginger and serve immediately, with the warm compote on the side.

Chocolate Risotto Pudding

*M*y good friend Jim Pallotta is a risotto freak. His ideal meal is risotto for an appetizer and risotto for the main course. When he begged me for a dessert risotto, we came up with this one. Thanks, Jim, it's a keeper.

SERVES 6 TO 8

½ cup coarsely chopped walnuts (optional)
2 tablespoons unsalted butter
2 cups superfino arborio rice
1 vanilla bean, split
4 cups water
2 cups whole milk
2 cups light or heavy cream
4 large egg yolks
½ cup white sugar
Grated zest and juice of 1 orange
2 tablespoons Grand Marnier
6 ounces semisweet chocolate, chopped
½ cup raisins (optional)
Whipped cream, for garnish
Fresh mint sprigs, for garnish

Place the nuts, if using, in a large skillet over medium heat and cook, shaking or stirring occasionally, until the nuts are brown, about 3 to 5 minutes. Set aside.

Melt the butter in a large straight-sided nonreactive saucepan over medium heat. Stir in the rice until coated.

Add the vanilla bean and 1 cup of water and cook, stirring constantly, until the liquid is absorbed by the rice. Continue adding the water, 1 cup at a time, stirring until it has been absorbed by the rice. Gradually add the milk, 1 cup at a time, and cook, stirring constantly, until the milk has been absorbed and the rice is al dente, about 18 to 20 minutes in all. Remove the vanilla bean.

Meanwhile, place the cream, egg yolks, and sugar in a medium-size mixing bowl and stir until very smooth, being sure to get rid of any lumps. Stir the mixture into the rice, then stir in the orange zest, orange juice, and Grand Marnier and cook, stirring, until the liquid has been absorbed. Add the chocolate and continue to stir until it is melted and incorporated. Add the raisins if desired.

Sprinkle with the chopped walnuts, if desired, and garnish with whipped cream and fresh mint. Serve warm or at room temperature.

BISCOTTI

$\mathcal{I}$f you want a surefire biscotti recipe, this is it. However, be forewarned that the recipe makes thinner than usual biscotti because I think the best are delicate rather than chunky and heavy. Feel free to change the kind of nuts or add bits of chocolate.

You can make the dough ahead of time and freeze or refrigerate it until you're ready to bake it.

MAKES 48 TO 50 BISCOTTI

⅓ to ½ cup roughly chopped toasted almonds
1¾ cups all-purpose flour
¾ teaspoon baking soda
¾ teaspoon baking powder
½ teaspoon kosher salt
½ cup (1 stick) unsalted butter, at room temperature
1 cup white sugar
2 small (or 1½ large) eggs
1 teaspoon grated lemon zest
1 teaspoon grated orange zest
1½ teaspoons vanilla extract

Preheat the oven to 350 degrees. Lightly butter a cookie sheet.

Combine the almonds, flour, baking soda, baking powder, and salt in a medium-size mixing bowl.

In a large bowl, cream the butter and sugar. Add the eggs, one at a time, beating well after each addition. Add the lemon and orange zests and the vanilla extract.

Add the almond mixture and mix well to combine. (It will feel much stickier and wetter than regular cookie dough.)

Form the dough into two 8-inch logs. Place on the cookie sheet, with at least 2 inches between them, and bake until the logs are just beginning to get golden, about 20 to 25 minutes. Remove from the oven and let cool slightly. (Leave the oven on.) This step can be done 1 week ahead.

When the logs are cool enough to handle, thinly slice on the diagonal into ⅜-inch slices.

Lay the biscotti on ungreased baking sheets, return them to the oven, and bake until crisp and golden brown, about 5 minutes on each side.

Let cool on racks and store in an airtight container.

STRAWBERRY RHUBARB CRUMBLE

*T*his classic combination of strawberries and rhubarb is the essence of spring, but you can make it any time of year by varying the type of fruit. It's especially good made with peaches and apples. Resist the temptation to add more sugar and, instead, let the tart rhubarb flavor shine through.

SERVES 6 TO 8

CRUMBLE TOPPING:
½ cup (1 stick) unsalted butter, at room temperature
⅔ cup lightly packed brown sugar
1 cup coarsely chopped pecans
1 cup all-purpose flour
1 cup rolled oats
¼ teaspoon ground cinnamon
¼ teaspoon kosher salt
Pinch of baking powder

1 pound fresh rhubarb, trimmed, halved lengthwise, and chopped
1 quart fresh strawberries, hulled and halved
1 tablespoon all-purpose flour
1 tablespoon plus 1 teaspoon white sugar
1 teaspoon fresh lemon juice

Preheat the oven to 250 degrees.

To make the topping: Place the butter and sugar in a medium-size mixing bowl and blend just until smooth. Add the pecans, flour, oats, cinnamon, salt, and baking powder and mix until creamy.

Spread the mixture evenly on an ungreased 8 × 11-inch baking sheet and bake about 15 minutes. Turn the pan and bake until golden, about 20 minutes more. Let cool.

Place the rhubarb and strawberries in a large bowl and toss with the 1 tablespoon flour and the lemon juice. Spread evenly on the baking sheet and bake until tender, about 30 minutes.

Crumble the topping over the warm strawberry mixture and serve immediately.

MANGO-RASPBERRY GRANITA

*M*angoes are my favorite fruit. I love having some of this granita in the freezer for those times I need a little bite of something sweet after dinner.

SERVES 4

1 cup water
½ cup fresh orange juice
2 teaspoons rice syrup (available at health food stores), honey, or white sugar
1 teaspoon vanilla extract
3 ripe mangoes, diced
1 medium-ripe to overripe banana, diced
1 pint fresh raspberries

Place the water, orange juice, rice syrup, and vanilla extract in a medium-size saucepan and bring to a boil over high heat. Add the mangoes and banana and cook until the mangoes are soft and all the liquid has been absorbed, about 10 minutes. Set aside to cool.

Place the mixture in a blender and blend until smooth. Add the raspberries by hand. Place the mixture in a baking pan and place in the freezer until solid, at least 2 hours. Scoop out of the pan with an ice cream scoop or a spoon and serve immediately.

DOUBLE LEMON TART

*S*o tart it almost hurts.

SERVES 8

CORNMEAL CRUST:
½ cup (1 stick) unsalted butter, at room temperature
¼ cup white sugar
1 large egg yolk
¾ cup all-purpose flour
¼ cup cornstarch
¼ cup stone-ground yellow cornmeal

LEMON FILLING:
Finely grated zest and juice of 2 lemons
4 large eggs
¾ cup white sugar
¾ cup heavy cream

LEMON CURD:
1 large egg
4 large egg yolks
½ cup white sugar
⅓ cup fresh lemon juice (about 1½ lemons)
1 tablespoon plus 2 teaspoons unsalted butter, cut into small pieces
1 cup fresh raspberries or blueberries, for garnish

To make the crust: Place the butter and sugar in a bowl and cream with a wooden spoon just until combined, being careful not to overbeat. Add the yolk, then the remaining crust ingredients, and beat just until the dough holds together, being careful not to overmix.

On a lightly floured surface, roll out the dough to a ¼-inch-thick round. Line a 9-inch tart pan with the dough. Refrigerate for at least 30 minutes.

Preheat the oven to 350 degrees.

Line the tart shell with aluminum foil and fill with raw beans or pie weights. Place in the oven and bake for 10 minutes. Remove the foil and beans and bake until the dough starts to turn golden brown, about 10 minutes. Remove from the oven and let cool.

To make the lemon filling: Preheat the oven to 325 degrees. Place the lemon zest and juice, eggs, sugar, and heavy cream in a bowl and beat until smooth. Pour into the prebaked shell and bake until the filling is set, about 30 minutes. Set aside to cool.

To make the lemon curd: Place the egg, egg yolks, sugar, and lemon juice in the top of a double boiler over simmering water. Whisk continuously until the mixture begins to thicken, about 2 to 3 minutes. Gradually whisk in the butter, one piece at a time, until it is completely incorporated. Set aside to cool.

When the lemon curd is cool, pour over the cooled lemon filling and spread evenly.

Let sit for 20 minutes, or refrigerate for up to 24 hours. Garnish with fresh raspberries or blueberries. Serve warm or cold.

PAN-FRIED APPLE TART WITH BASIL, LEMON, AND WALNUTS

*T*his tart falls in line with the way I like to make desserts—free-form, rustic, and homey. The unusual addition of basil lends a hint of anise flavor.

SERVES 6 TO 8

DOUGH:
2¾ cups all-purpose flour
¾ cup white sugar
½ cup walnuts, finely ground
1 cup (2 sticks) unsalted butter, chilled and thinly sliced
2 large eggs
2 large egg yolks
l teaspoon vanilla extract
Grated zest of 1 lemon
1 teaspoon fresh lemon juice

FILLING:
1 cup raisins
¼ cup Calvados or applejack
3 tablespoons unsalted butter
5 cups peeled and roughly chopped Granny Smith, McIntosh, or Macoun apples
1 cup lightly packed dark brown sugar
Grated zest and juice of 1 lemon
2 cinnamon sticks
1 cup toasted walnuts, finely chopped
1 tablespoon cornstarch
1 tablespoon cold water
½ cup chopped fresh basil leaves

To make the dough: Place the flour, sugar, and walnuts in a mixing bowl. Add the butter and, with your hands, mix until the butter has been completely incorporated. Add the eggs, egg yolks, vanilla, and lemon zest and juice. Mix with a spoon or by hand until the dough forms a ball. Divide the dough in half and shape into two disks. Cover with plastic wrap and refrigerate for at least 30 minutes.

Preheat the oven to 375 degrees.

To make the filling: Place the nuts in a large skillet over medium heat and cook, shaking or stirring occasionally, until the nuts are brown, about 3 to 5 minutes. Place the raisins and Calvados in a small bowl and set aside until the raisins are plumped. Melt 2 tablespoons butter in a large skillet over medium heat. Add the apples, brown sugar, lemon zest and juice, cinnamon sticks, and walnuts, stirring well after each addition. Cook until the apples are golden brown, about 10 minutes. Discard the cinnamon sticks. Place the cornstarch and water in a small bowl and stir to dissolve the cornstarch. Add the mixture to the apples and cook, stirring occasionally, until the mixture comes to a boil. Off the heat, add the basil, the reserved raisins, and the Calvados.

To assemble the tart, divide the dough into 2 pieces. On a floured surface, roll each piece into a 9-inch circle. Melt the remaining butter in an oven-proof 9-inch skillet over medium heat and place one of the dough circles in it. Cook for 2 minutes, then add the apple mixture, spreading it evenly over the dough. Place the remaining circle over the apple mixture and seal the edges together with the tines of a fork. Cook for 3 to 4 minutes, shaking the pan occasionally to be sure the dough is not sticking.

Transfer the pan to the oven and bake until the tart is golden brown on the bottom, about 10 minutes. Remove the pan from the oven. Flip the tart over very carefully onto a flat plate and slide it back into the pan. (This is not an easy maneuver; if you break it, just call it a crumble.) Return the tart to the oven and cook until the other side is golden, about 10 minutes more.

Transfer the tart to a serving dish and let sit for 10 minutes. Serve warm.

BRICK-OVEN CHERRY TART WITH WHITE CHOCOLATE AND MASCARPONE

*O*ne of my favorite desserts, this tart is incredibly rich but not overly sweet. The white chocolate gives the tart a wonderful vanilla-y backbone and the mascarpone adds just enough flavor and texture to marry all the ingredients. At Olives, we bake this in a brick oven, but it will turn out just as well in your home oven.

SERVES 4

TART DOUGH:
1⅓ cups all-purpose flour
6 tablespoons white or powdered sugar
¼ cup ground walnuts
½ cup (1 stick) unsalted butter, chilled and thinly sliced
1 large egg
1 large egg yolk
½ teaspoon vanilla extract
Grated zest of ½ orange
½ teaspoon fresh lemon juice

FILLING:
3 tablespoons mascarpone
1½ ounces white chocolate, chopped
½ cup pitted fresh Bing cherries
1 tablespoon chopped almonds

To make the dough: Place the flour, sugar, and walnuts in a medium-size mixing bowl. Add the butter and, with your hands, mix until the butter has been completely incorporated. Add the egg, egg yolk, vanilla, orange zest, and lemon juice. Mix with a spoon or by hand until the dough forms a ball. Cover with plastic wrap and refrigerate for at least 30 minutes.

Preheat the oven to 450 degrees.

Roll the dough out on a floured surface to a 9- to 10-inch circle. Fold the edges over and crimp them with the tines of a fork. Place the tart on a baking sheet and spread the mascarpone over the dough. Sprinkle with the white chocolate, cherries, and almonds. Place in the oven and bake until the chocolate has melted and the cherries are warmed, about 15 minutes.

Serve warm or at room temperature.

PUMPKIN BREAD PUDDING WITH CARAMEL SAUCE AND WHIPPED CREAM

*C*omfort food your mother never thought of. Rich and spicy.

SERVES 6 TO 8

5 to 6 cups 2-inch cubes brioche or challah bread, toasted
3 cups heavy cream
3 cups milk
1 tablespoon ground cinnamon
½ teaspoon ground nutmeg
Pinch of allspice
Pinch of kosher salt
½ cup honey or lightly packed brown sugar
4 large eggs
4 large egg yolks
1 teaspoon vanilla extract
*1 16-ounce can pumpkin puree (*not *pumpkin pie filling)*

CARAMEL SAUCE:
1 cup white sugar
½ cup water
½ cup heavy cream
2 tablespoons unsalted butter, at room temperature

¾ cup heavy cream
1 teaspoon vanilla extract

Preheat the oven to 350 degrees. Lightly butter an 8 x 8-inch baking pan.

Place the bread cubes in the prepared pan.

Place the cream and milk in a large saucepan and bring to a boil over medium-high heat. Off the heat, stir in the cinnamon, nutmeg, allspice, salt, honey, eggs, egg yolks, vanilla, and pumpkin. Pour over the bread and gently stir to combine.

Place the baking pan in a roasting pan filled with enough water to come halfway up the sides of the baking pan. Bake until the pudding is set, about 35 minutes.

While the pudding is baking, make the caramel sauce: Place the sugar and water in a small saucepan over high heat and cook, stirring, until the sugar is dissolved. Then cook, without stirring, washing down the sides of the pan with a pastry brush dipped in water, until the syrup has turned the color of caramel, about 15 minutes. Take the syrup off the heat, let it cool slightly, then slowly add the 1/2 cup cream and the butter, being careful that the hot syrup doesn't spatter, and stir until smooth.

Place a stainless-steel or copper mixing bowl in the freezer for 5 minutes. Remove the bowl and add the 3/4 cup cream. Beat the cream with a whisk until it forms soft peaks. Gradually add the vanilla extract. Refrigerate until ready to serve.

While the pudding is still warm, scoop it into bowls and drizzle with the caramel sauce. Top with the whipped cream and serve immediately.

MAIL-ORDER SOURCES

CAVIAR, FOIE GRAS, FLAVORED OILS:

BOYAJIAN, INC.
349 Lenox Street
Norwood, MA 02062
800-419-4677

CAVIAR, CHESTNUT FLOUR, CHORIZO, DUCK FAT, FOIE
GRAS, POMEGRANATE MOLASSES, SPICES, TRUFFLES,
TRUFFLE OIL:

DEAN AND DELUCA
560 Broadway
New York, NY 10012
800-221-7714

SPICES:

PENZEY'S
P.O. Box 1448
Waukesha, WI 53187
414-574-0277

INDEX

METRIC EQUIVALENCIES

LIQUID AND DRY MEASURE EQUIVALENCIES

CUSTOMARY	METRIC
¼ teaspoon	1.25 milliliters
½ teaspoon	2.5 milliliters
1 teaspoon	5 milliliters
1 tablespoon	15 milliliters
1 fluid ounce	30 milliliters
¼ cup	60 milliliters
⅓ cup	80 milliliters
½ cup	120 milliliters
1 cup	240 milliliters
1 pint (*2 cups*)	480 milliliters
1 quart (*4 cups, 32 ounces*)	960 milliliters (*.96 liter*)
1 gallon (*4 quarts*)	3.84 liters
1 ounce (*by weight*)	28 grams
¼ pound (*4 ounces*)	114 grams
1 pound (*16 ounces*)	454 grams
2.2 pounds	1 kilogram (*1000 grams*)

OVEN TEMPERATURE EQUIVALENCIES

DESCRIPTION	°FAHRENHEIT	°CELSIUS
Cool	200	90
Very slow	250	120
Slow	300–325	150–160
Moderately slow	325–350	160–180
Moderate	350–375	180–190
Moderately hot	375–400	190–200
Hot	400–450	200–230
Very hot	450–500	230–260